Radical Curriculum Theory Reconsidered

A Historical Approach

Radical Curriculum Theory Reconsidered

A Historical Approach

Peter S. Hlebowitsh

FOREWORD BY DANIEL TANNER

Teachers College, Columbia University
New York and London

Published by Teachers College Press, 1234 Amsterdam Avenue, New York, NY 10027

For reprint permission, grateful acknowledgment is made to: *Journal of Curriculum Studies, Educational Theory, Science Education, Journal of Educational Thought, Curriculum Inquiry,* and *Equity and Excellence.*

Library of Congress Cataloging-in-Publication Data

Hlebowitsh, Peter S.
   Radical curriculum theory reconsidered : a historical approach / Peter S. Hlebowitsh ; foreword by Daniel Tanner.
      p.   cm.
   Includes bibliographical references and index.
   ISBN 0-8077-3276-1.—ISBN 0-8077-3275-3 (pbk.)
   1. Curriculum planning—United States.   2. Education—United States—Curricula.   3. Curriculum change—United. States.   1. Title.
LB2806.15.H57   1993
375'.001—dc20   93-8615

Printed on acid-free paper
Manufactured in the United States of America
99 98 97 96 95 94 93   7 6 5 4 3 2 1

Contents

In Memoriam

Paul S. Hlebowitsh
(1962–1986)

Foreword

Over the years, whenever my students express pessimism over the chasm between the ideals of American democracy and what seems to them to be nothing short of an impenetrable ignorance on the part of the American populace, I call their attention to the words of Georges Sorel: "Can you imagine anything more horrible than government by professors!"

The radical academic Left of today, who grew out of the student protest movement of the 1960s and early 1970s, gained a secure and strong presence in our colleges and universities during the 1980s. But where the causes of their student days were allied with action in the real world, such as the opposition to the Vietnam war, their causes today are more safely confined to theory—critical theory, deconstruction, revisionism, neo-Marxism, and so on. And where so many of the leading experimentalist-progressives during the first half of the twentieth century—such as John Dewey, Harold Alberty, Paul Hanna, Ralph Tyler, and Hilda Taba—addressed the practical problems of curriculum development, and actually helped to develop curriculum materials and designs, today's radical academic Left hold themselves aloof from such engagement. When not portraying the role of the school as inconsequential, they have proceeded to portray the teacher as an unwitting accomplice to a scheme for promoting "cultural reproduction" or "social control"—as opposed to "emancipation" of the masses. And they have proceeded to identify John Dewey as forging the theoretical underpinnings for such "reproduction" and "control."

Wracked by a crisis of internal theoretical contradictions, the collapse of the Soviet Union, and the decline of Marxism, and coupled with the clarion call for democracy throughout the world, the radical academic Left have had to regroup and reinvent their rationales, doctrines, and heroes. Thus they have rehabilitated John Dewey. But in doing so, they have reincarnated Dewey as a radical liberal or radical reconstructionist. They conveniently overlook Dewey's criticism of reconstructionism as indoctrination, and they fail to share Dewey's abiding faith in popular education as the bulwark of the American democratic prospect—a faith so passionately shared by his fellow experimentalists.

Peter Hlebowitsh has written a compelling account of the radical academic Left in the curriculum field. He has sought to find the positive aspects of challenging the heritage of a field and, hence, possibly bringing a new vitality to that field. He raises critical questions about the failure of the curriculum field to build on its rich and powerful heritage of accomplishments and to learn from its misguided turns, as well as to counter the flock mentality that finds educators alternately and repeatedly embracing and discarding the very same innovations, changes, and reforms like changing fads and fashions. At the same time, he has also exposed the doctrinaire cast of so many of the radical academic Left and the authoritarian stance taken in aligning themselves, wittingly or unwittingly, with those on the political Right in disparaging popular education, in creating false categories for those experimentalist-progressives who contributed so significantly to the field, and in revising the historic record so as to give credence to their doctrines. He exposes the negativism that pervades the radical academic Left in finding failure in our schools while avoiding responsible action for curriculum construction and revitalization in the real world of the public school. He has pointed to the failure of the radical academic Left to match their condemnations with constructive proposals, to formulate effective means to meet their professed democratic ends. This is contrasted against the commitment by the experimentalist-progressives to test ideas in practice, to seek the best available evidence as the guide for practical application, and to see constructive solutions to problems through reflective intelligence as opposed to doctrine, fad, dictum, conformity, or mere tradition.

The issues examined by Peter Hlebowitsh are not merely "academic"; they have far-reaching implications for school and society. For example, the radical academic Left have become strange bedfellows with the conservative Right in attacking the cosmopolitan, comprehensive high school. For the radical academic Left, the comprehensive high school is synonymous with curriculum tracking and with promoting antidemocratic social separation and discrimination. These antidemocratic functions are seen by the radical academic Left as intentional outcomes of the *Cardinal Principles* report of 1918, whereas the document itself repeatedly and pervasively called for a comprehensive curriculum to serve a cosmopolitan population in a no-track school. The radical academic Left and the conservative Right have become allies in supporting a one-track secondary school geared to the standard academic curriculum. They have ignored the realities whereby the college-bound population in such a general academic secondary school proceeds to pursue the advanced academic courses, leaving more than half of the population in an "undertrack."

In more recent years, the radical academic Left have either remained strangely silent regarding the ominous antidemocratic prospects of "schools of choice" (alternative schools and the use of public funds for tuition vouchers), or they have been allied with the conservative Right in supporting such "alternative schools." In so doing, they have become a party to a scheme that would redirect public funds to support special-interest schools for special-interest constituencies. America's great pluralism would find no common ground through the school. Instead of seeking a sense of unity through diversity, the schools would be divided in form, function, and the social origins and destinations of the pupil populations.

With insightful and incisive scholarship, Peter Hlebowitsh has carefully and fairly exposed the issues and problems; he has also examined the implications not only for the curriculum field but also for the wider school and society. He has undertaken a work of scholarship that few young scholars in the field would have ventured, considering the influential and, in many respects, dominant orthodoxy gained by the radical academic Left in the social and philosophical foundations of education.

In the strongest tradition of democratic theory and practice, as orchestrated by leading experimentalist-progressives in our century, Peter Hlebowitsh makes the case for the democratizing function of the cosmopolitan school in a pluralist society. As the twentieth century draws to a close, worldwide events give evidence that the experimentalist-progressives were indeed on the side of history.

Daniel Tanner
Rutgers University

Acknowledgments

In the course of writing this book, I have benefited from the support of many people who have assisted me out of both the spirit of friendship and the stirrings of professional conviction. After offering some criticism of a paper that I presented at the 1990 meeting of the American Educational Research Association, George Willis was among the first to encourage me to expand on an unsystematic critique that would eventually become the basis for this book. The actual formation of the book's thesis, however, was originally fashioned quite some time ago in Daniel Tanner's graduate seminar at Rutgers University and has since been nurtured through continuing conversation with various colleagues. Professor Tanner deserves credit for influencing many of the ideas in this book, particularly the first part of the last chapter, which deals with the issue of school choice. Since some of the ideas in this book were tested at recent conferences of the American Educational Research Association and in various publications, I have also been able to garner quite a few suggestions and criticisms, including gracious responses from William Pinar and Ralph Tyler. I thank all of the above-named scholars.

The four years that I have now spent at the University of Houston have also contributed to my work. I should like to thank Dennis Fehr for his editorial advice on this work and acknowledge the overall support offered by my "curriculum" colleagues, Al Warner and Laurel Tanner, and my ever-supportive friends, Lane Roy Gauthier and David Yaden.

There is also a rather long list of faithful colleagues who engaged in the onerous task of reading a preliminary draft of the book. Their reactions, as anticipated, were remarkably helpful. I simply cannot thank them enough. This group included Richard Gibboney, University of Pennsylvania; Paul Theobald, Texas A&M University; Edmund Short, Pennsylvania State University; Daniel Tanner, Rutgers University; and the anonymous reviewers of Teachers College Press. I also cannot forget all the helpful conversations held with my friends back East, particularly my colleagues at Long Island

University, Betty Sichel and Anthony DeFalco, and my irrepressible writing partner, William Wraga. Of course, I should also like to thank my editor, Brian Ellerbeck, for recognizing my work and advising me on its proper direction. I feel quite lucky to have worked with an editor whose considerable language skills are equal to his basis of understanding in the field of curriculum studies.

Of course, my greatest debt of gratitude goes to my family, particularly to my children, who have endured the daily ritual of finding me preoccupied with the matters of this manuscript and other work-related issues. Too often they have looked to me for engagement, frequently loaded down with the materials for a wide agenda of fun and games, only to be disappointed. Fortunately, their mother has been much more responsible. Thanks goes out to all of them: my children—Margaret, Paul, Nadia, and Nikolai—and my wife, Erica Born-Hlebowitsh.

Finally, a word or two about my brother, Paul Hlebowitsh, who died tragically in the full bloom of youth, in the midst of a life marked by social responsibility, professional commitment, and an encompassing sense of joy. This book is dedicated to his memory and to the enduring belief that from tragedy spring empowering forces known to those who can find and cultivate them.

Introduction

The field of curriculum covers a broad territory, encompassing all the thinking that influences the content, organization, and overall character of learning experiences, especially as they have been justified under the auspices of the school. As a result, the actual identification of a knowledge base for curriculum is often difficult. Claims of a "paradigm" for curriculum inquiry (Tanner & Tanner, 1980), for instance, exist side by side with arguments that view the curriculum field as a mythology (Egan, 1978), or, in the interpretation of many radical critics, as on the boundaries of obsolescence (Huebner, 1976; Pinar, 1978).

Today one can find several different accounts of the main historical purposes and practices that led to the organization of curriculum as a formal area of study. Similarly, one can find conflicting historical characterizations of well-known curriculum figures, including, to name a few, John Dewey, Hollis Caswell, Jesse Newlon, Harold Rugg, Ralph Tyler, and Hilda Taba. Tyler, for instance, has been described, on the one hand, as an advocate of social efficiency and the exercise of behavioristic manipulations in the curriculum (Apple, 1979; Kliebard, 1975b; Pinar, 1975) and, on the other hand, as a Deweyan who abhorred the efficiency-driven curriculum tactics he is portrayed by others as supporting (Tanner & Tanner, 1980). Similarly, Dewey has been described as an egalitarian responsive to the social causes of justice and equality (Kliebard, 1986; McLaren, 1989) and as an instrumentalist who was insensibly wedded to the idea of adjusting the individual to "fit" into society (Grumet, 1981; Karier, 1976; Katz, 1971). Caswell, Newlon, and Taba have each been interpreted as committed progressive-experimentalists and, alternatively, as committed advocates of social efficiency and social control. Given these differences, it is fair to say that there is considerable controversy over the chief assumptions and tenets underpinning curriculum theory, development, history, and criticism.

Yet there are enough commonalities to allow for the publication of several scholarly journals devoted to the field of curriculum, as well as the publication of a handful of scholarly synoptic textbooks (Schubert, 1986; Tanner & Tanner, 1980). The proliferation of doctoral programs dedicated to curriculum theory and curriculum development within schools of education, as well as the identification of curriculum studies as a research division in the American Educational Research Association, also speaks to there being some overall structure. Despite its expansive character, the field of curriculum has a sense of commonality that is vested in its diversity and in the understanding that there are no complete and final answers to the complex problems inherent in discussing what should be taught, how it should be taught, and why it should be taught. Unfortunately, the diversity in the field has often fragmented into allegiances, leading inevitably to some of the opposing viewpoints discussed in this work.

This book is not a history of curriculum thought but an effort to track the controversial issues inherent in the variety of interpretations that curriculum scholars have produced about their own area of study. The recent emergence of a group of scholars dedicated to reconceptualizing the field makes this a particularly relevant, if not necessary, exercise. These scholars have offered radically different methods of viewing, analyzing, and interpreting issues relevant to the school curriculum. They have called for a new level of variance in the discourse of curriculum studies, arguing strongly for the inclusion of themes from political analysis, aesthetic criticism, phenomenology, and feminist studies. Their hope has been that the airing of these perspectives in the scholarly discourse will sharpen new visions of the problems and purposes of the school curriculum. Some of this hope has been fulfilled, since a robust level of dissonance now exists in the field.

All, however, is not as it might appear. The current radical analysis of the curriculum field, while embracing the idea of diversity, has also called for the demise of the so-called dominant curriculum perspective. The case against this more moderate perspective is built on a historical foundation that has been distorted to support the fixed belief that schools serve the ends of social and economic oppression, and has in turn led to the promotion of reductionist views on curriculum history as it relates to the broad themes of social control, American pragmatism, the progressive-experimentalist tradition, and the role of ideology in curriculum development.

The major theoretical shift in the field proposed by many radicals thinkers aims to fill the space created by the demise of the dominant Tylerian view, which they presume to be rooted in the operations of social efficiency and social control. Prominent among these thinkers is William Pinar, who has confidently associated the obsolescence of the Tyler rationale with the pronounced rise in the reconceptualization of the field. According to Pinar:

> Tylerian dominance has passed. Like a disappearing star in another galaxy it takes some years for everyone, depending upon his or her location, to see this. The fact is that to a remarkable extent reconceptualization has occurred. (1988, p. 8)

In some ways, such a statement represents the worst of the modern radical analysis because it stakes out one ideological ground as correct and the other as anachronistic. To dismiss as obsolete a highly significant and ongoing body of curriculum scholarship, one that has a long history of discourse rooted in the progressive-experimentalism of Dewey, and to support a radicalized form of scholarship as most worthwhile, is to engage in a form of tyranny that draws a firm line between what is good and what is bad in curriculum studies. The purpose of this book is to provide a critique of curriculum radicalism that helps to rescue the progressive curriculum perspective from the charges leveled against it and, in doing so, to advance new lines of debate for the continued development of the curriculum field.

Radical Curriculum Theory Reconsidered

A Historical Approach

CHAPTER 1

THE RECONCEPTUALIZATION OF THE CURRICULUM FIELD

> Change becomes significant of new possibilities and ends to be attained; it becomes prophetic of a better future. Change is associated with progress rather than with lapse or fall.
>
> John Dewey

The field of curriculum theory and development emerged out of a pragmatic intellectual tradition that brought the scientific method, philosophical empiricism, and the democratic ideal into one stream of educational thought. As a progressive-experimentalist, John Dewey articulated many of the early ideas in this area by speaking directly to the idea of curriculum as an inquiry process and by offering a practical framework against which educational formulations could be examined (Tanner & Tanner, 1980). Dewey's influence in the curriculum field, however, was buffeted by other prominent voices, many of which gave rise to movements that became more influential in the world of practice than any that had their source in Dewey (Kliebard, 1986).

The conflicting perspectives represented in these movements have persisted. Among modern-day curriculum scholars, fundamental disagreements exist over practical concerns of construction as well as over theoretical issues of philosophical and historical interpretation. A direct challenge, in fact, has been offered to the view that the development of the curriculum field was a progressive effort to replace the heavy hand of formalism in the school with a vision of democratic schooling. In the reinterpretation of many radical commentators, the historical foundations of the curriculum field are built on administrative and managerial imperatives that have exalted the role of efficiency and rationality in the organization and overall implementation of the school curriculum. Increasingly, these scholars have taken the view that curriculum study is rooted in the soil of social control and cultural consensus (Apple, 1979; Franklin, 1986; Pinar, 1978) and that a wholesale reconceptualization of the field is thus in order.

Curriculum studies encompasses a wide range of concerns and philosophical orientations. This has been the case since its inception as a formal area of inquiry during the early decades of the twentieth century. Progressive-experimentalists such as John Dewey (1902a, 1916) and Boyd Bode (1927, 1938b) raised serious questions about the traditional conduct of schooling and worked directly to secure a foundation for new progressive possibilities in the school. George Counts (1932) employed a social-class analysis in his writing that led to a call for the school to address pervasive social ills in ways that would lead to the reconstruction of the social order. Franklin Bobbitt (1918, 1924) and W. W. Charters (1924) formulated curriculum strategies built on the idea of teaching youth their roles in adult life through a process that was technocratic in orientation and devoid of the sociocivic flavor so clear in the work of Dewey and several other prominent progressives. During these early years, there was also a vital Herbartian movement, which sought synthesis in the content of curriculum; a considerable drive for child-centered learning, which sought to make the schools more joyful and experiential; and impressive numbers of committed social-efficiency experts, such as David Snedden (1914), who wanted to design the school to act as an agency for the social predestination of youth. The diversity of thought in the field, in fact, bordered on divisiveness, moving Harold Rugg (1927), under the sponsorship of the National Society for the Study of Education, to edit a yearbook dedicated to acknowledging differences in the field and to searching for new bases of professional commonality and community.

Current radical commentators in the curriculum field, however, by focusing only on certain facets of early curriculum thought while ignoring others, have falsely reduced most of the curriculum tradition to a scheme for social control. They see the field as defined by Bobbitt and Charters, with a contemporary legacy anchored in a highly behavioristic portrayal of the Tyler rationale. American pragmatism has been virtually ignored in the critique, except to be occasionally misinterpreted as a positivist movement. Similarly, the Deweyan perspective on experimentalism has received little substantive attention, though it too has been distorted. Giroux (1988a), for instance, like many other radical critics, has failed to acknowledge Dewey's instrumentalism and continues to present Dewey as a social reconstructionist. This problem is embedded in Giroux's broader misrepresentation of instrumentalism as a conservative force in the curriculum field (Bowers, 1987). At the same time, much of the radical critique reflects a Eurocentric literature based in the Frankfort School—a particular irony, given the radical penchant for bashing the so-called Eurocentric cultural imperialism in the public schools. In its effort to find the expression of voice among the marginalized in the public schools, much of the radical element in curriculum studies has seemingly forgotten about the distinct American voice in the constitution of the American public schools that, by virtually all accounts, established the early record for the democratization of schooling in the industrial nations of the world, including, of course, marxist societies.

All of this has been accompanied by a broader argument against the historical positioning of positivism in the construction of the curriculum. Positivism, in this regard, is seen by the radicals as rationality gone awry, as representing the so-called objective science often used to justify school operations. In the context of the curriculum, positivism is seen as leading to the construction of a school world disengaged from social analysis, cultural struggle, revolutionary possibility, and forms of understanding that reflect the lives of those who have been historically oppressed. In the context of human affairs, positivism is perceived as seriously flawed by its failure to see "facts" as socially conceived constructs and to deal critically with its own ideological underpinnings. Thus, say the radicals, positivism must be exposed as the great pretender of truth, the projection of science as scientism—the methodological cover for a political conservativism that seeks to maintain the status quo. In the schools, it is the rationale for imposing a programmatic version of learning and teaching that advantages only those who might benefit from a politically conservative agenda.

Having thus diagnosed the insidious positivist influences in the curriculum, various radical scholars have called for a leftist awakening to palliate the tradition of control in the curriculum and, in the long run, to reconstruct curriculum studies in a manner that transcends the traditional regard for procedural design. This process is to begin by asking new questions about the underlying rationales and ideologies that support the knowledge, learning patterns, organizational structures, and evaluative mechanisms used in schools. Hermeneutic interpretation, political critique, gender and social-class analysis, and phenomenological inquiry are all believed to be needed, since without them curriculum studies will fail to take account of neglected areas in gender, race, class, and culture inquiry.

The call to widen the analytical sights of curriculum scholarship is, in one sense, appropriate. During the past decade, Pinar (1975, 1988) and others have helped to bring a new vitality to curriculum interpretation by stressing philosophical perspectives that generally have not been part of historical discussions on the school curriculum. The problem, however, is that there is a certain authoritarian cast to the so-called new perspective that inscribes one ideology as correct while systematically attacking those not in ideological conformity as objectionable or disgracefully traditional, technocratic, or positivistic. Thus, despite talk about a dialectic (an openly oppositional viewpoint that questions *all* assumptions), there is an unproblematic context to much of the radical argumentation. For instance, the assumption that the curriculum field is marked by efforts to control, oppress, and retard is not open to question; it is a given that is preliminary to the radical solution of liberation and emancipation. Such an argument is not questioned, although increasingly there is acknowledgment that it may be overly deterministic. As we shall see, much distortion results from this stance. During the formative phases of the curriculum field (when it was influenced by, among others, Dewey, Bode, and Rugg), the intent of curriculum formulations was not to find ways of controlling individuals through the institution of schooling, as has been alleged, but to find ways of cultivating the skills and knowledge that individuals needed in order to control their own destinies and the collective destinies of their communities and society. This was as much a matter of individual growth and development as it was collective or group growth.

CRITICAL THEORY AND THE CURRICULUM

Many of the contemporary challenges in curriculum studies have been inspired by a critical theory of education. Over the past decade or so, those working out of such a perspective have offered interesting analyses of class interest and so-called cultural hegemony in the school. Disclosures of widespread injustice and inequity within various facets of school practice (including areas such as tracking, vocational education, special education, and teacher education) have abounded. The interpretations offered by those informed by critical theory have also stressed, among other things, the power of individual initiative, the recognition of human intention, the unmasking of commonsense assumptions as ideology, the description of social-control mechanisms in the school (e.g., pupil testing as a form of surveillance, special education as a covert form of social control), and the general assumption that society is marked by conflicting interests of class, gender, and culture (Gibson, 1986). We now turn to a description of these themes.

Critical theory in education aims to disclose all forms of injustice and inequality in schooling by revealing the interests served by the knowledge and the human action brought to bear in school settings. By probing into the ideological and political forces that underlie the workaday affairs of the school, critical theorists have created new and unconventional ways of looking at school phenomena.

Of course, even as they relate to curriculum studies, all critical theorists do not speak with one voice. Because there are considerable disparities and disagreements within critical theory, one cannot speak of it as one idea. Still, as a general construct, critical theory has a rough consensual outlook, which is rooted in the Frankfort School and anecdotally confirmed by the fact that a community of thinkers has loosely aligned itself to the term.

The influence of the Frankfort School in the development of a critical theory of education is towering. The scholarship conducted at the Institute for Social Research in Frankfort was aimed mainly at refuting the assumptions of positivism in the hope of revitalizing more radical forms of inquiry. According to this group, the act of theorizing had been usurped by the positivist tendency to treat reality with a system of rationality that had no moral commitment and no method of self-criticism. Thus positivist thought always failed to criticize the status quo and inevitably supported existing systems of powers (Horkheimer, 1972).

Critical theory starts where positivism never ventures. It touts itself as a process of critique that is neither neutral nor objective, but is profoundly negativistic and metaphysical. Negativity in critical theory is a philosophical pledge, consisting of the denial of what is accepted. Such a commitment is believed to preserve the dynamism of the lived experience through its respect for ambiguity and its promise to identify and destroy any elements that begin to solidify as rigidities of the establishment or status quo. Thus all conventions are subjected to ongoing inspection, criticism, and protest. What might be regarded as true or rational is more or less an open question, part and parcel of a dialectical process that necessitates continuing oppositional thought. Consequently, through negativity, truth and reason are denied the opportunity to take up residence as orthodoxies or conventions.

The struggle of the critical theorist, then, is largely a struggle against common sense and rationalist hubris. The world is not as we see it, and the day-to-day affairs of life cannot be entrusted to habit, routine, rule, custom, or reason. Faith in such matters represents a rejection of the process of negativity, which is thought to be essential to preserving our self-consciousness and our collective freedom.

In any civilization, constraints exist; some limitations on freedom create the semblance of control and order needed to maintain civilization. To the critical theorist, repression is the price that is paid for civilization. As Marcuse (1964) explained, there is a "surplus repression" that accompanies society, a one-dimensionality of life that moves humankind to find meaning in its own forms of technological and institutional domination. Workers, for instance, believing that their own interests are dependent on the success of the system, unwittingly advance the interests of the very forces that seek to enslave and exploit them. The result is a kind of cooptation that silences all voices of opposition or negation. Living in a one-dimensional society, individuals encounter no negating influence and have no contradictory version of reality; they become things, no longer sentient but rather instrumental and soulless. To identify humanity with its one-dimensional society is to disconnect persons from themselves, from the inner visions of life that fall victim to a homogeneous culture.

Given these influences, humanity must find an escape that overcomes the repressions of society. Part of this freedom, as mentioned earlier, is found in the dialectic, in the active questioning of everything that passes as truth or reason. There is also a search, however, for a teleology that gives meaning to human existence; at this point, critical theory moves toward an existential orientation (or what some have labeled as a postcritical theory), embracing the idea of engaging learners to look introspectively for a more authentic sense of self and sense of life. Pinar and Grumet (1981) have contributed to this pedagogical purpose by reconceiving the work of curriculum in its Latin verb form, *currere*, an idea that seeks to liberate the individual from the external structures of life through meditative pondering, intuitive comprehension, imagination, and an active as well as more penetrating interpretation of everyday events. More will be said about this later.

Critical theory in c
and imposition; it is ʳ
practice by revealiʳ
moved to think ᵃ᾿
have traditionaᴵ
theory prides ᾿
on disclosinᵍ
as commoʳ   8
lum, at eᴵ
latentlʸ
of youtʰ
phenomenoⁿ.
 By taking tʰ
field, critical theory ‿
cerns that bear directlʸ
the society. The ideal of traⁱⁿ
premium placed on building a n‿
tentially aware individual. The schoⁿ
cally to involve the transmitting of estaₗ
by critical theorists in a way that embracₑ
contradictions of life and seeks to "emancipate
they may gain more power over their own lives. An ᵥ
this emancipation process is to extricate the individuⁿ
ceived mechanical, procedural, and external compulsions. ⁱ ‿
from the many delimiting dimensions of schooling is said to a‿
the individual to achieve a more authentic personal identity.
 There is also a belief, however, that the individual needs to escape from the forces of rationality. As a result, critical theorists are wary of the methods of science, believing that science leads inexorably to scientism (the use of scientific instrumentality to cloak ideological phenomena). For instance, the construction of special education as an instructional category cannot be understood simply as the manifest and rational attempt to offer certain youngsters remedial and other opportunities for benevolent purposes; rather it is seen as a covert effort to sort and slot students in ways that oppress a disproportionate number of minority youngsters and those of low socioeconomic backgrounds. As an instructional endeavor, special education is legitimated by a science of test scores, research findings, and other objective data. But from the critical theory perspective, special education must be seen in terms of its less obvious effects, which might include acknowledging how children in such settings typically suffer psychological handicaps that ultimately

...ation of their academic competence and

...ansformation is fundamental in another
...eory does not accept the image of the com-
...algamating agency for society, a great deal of
... on criticizing the effort to use the school for
...cohesiveness and social harmony. To embrace the
...ing agency means to consent to the forces of social
...e effect of reproducing the status quo. Transforma-
... the other hand, is part of a cultural and political
... relies on an ongoing process of critique and self-
...ess. It obviously goes well beyond the walls of the school
...d the logic of the technocratic rationality that allegedly
...among the determiners of school policy and practice. By
...ng the political and ideological underpinnings of the curric-
..., critical theorists hope to establish conditions for more than
...room, or even curricular, change; they seek to go to the founda-
...ns of policy rationalizations and to the guiding philosophical or
...eological framework for schooling in the society. Many early progressives, of course, also shook at these foundations; but, in most
cases, they did so in the general belief that the school was the chief
agency for the reform of society and that change itself was an incremental process of reconstruction guided by the scientific method.

Curriculum theory has long been viewed as playing a formative
role in setting the boundaries of the school experience. The lesson
from the critical theorists, however, is that such a theory has an
inevitable blinding effect, a taken-for-granted legitimacy that over-
whelms the particularities of the lived experience and ultimately
supports an ideology of control rooted in economic and political
relationships. Boundaries, in this sense, are believed to be deleteri-
ous constraints that lend themselves to the positivist tendency to
reduce the world to axioms and universal truths.

The resistance to boundaries in the curriculum has led some to
accuse critical theory of promulgating criticism as theory (Tanner &
Tanner, 1979). The implication is that critical theory, while con-
veying an abiding commitment to the process of critique, generally
resists any formulation of methods or rationales that might provide
a handle for the mitigation of the very problems it exposes. This
raises an interesting point because, in a way, critical theory cannot
even hope to provide much insight on the actual constitution of the
school curriculum without compromising itself and becoming part
of the very structure that it seeks to overthrow. Since critical theory

is driven by the belief that relativity and subjectivity are unavoidable, and even desirable, consequences of curriculum practice, it faces a kind of crisis of reality in the arena of curriculum development. The effort to design a curriculum is openly rejected because to do so would require a crippling procedural consensus. However, to be useful in schools, curriculum development obviously has to have an overarching purpose and has to uphold some conscious environmental standard. The school, to borrow Dewey's phrase, represents a purified environment, deliberately conceived to produce an educative effect.

Yet there is general agreement among critical theorists that the work of curriculum theory must have practical implications. Critical theorists, though often criticized for failing to deal with practical concerns, will acknowledge the need to deal with questions concerning what should be taught, why it should be taught, and who will benefit. Their orientation is entirely abstract, however, containing no procedural guidance on how to give life to educative experiences. To teachers, whom they frequently cast as unthinking agents of capitalist interests, they give no specific counsel about actual undertakings in the classroom; they give only generalized "strategies" of counterhegemony, consciousness raising, and emancipatory action. The teacher's thinking can be informed only by the spirit of critical theory; there is no problem-focused design.

There is also a very strong emphasis on what has loosely been called the hidden curriculum—school actions that are justified by articulated intentions but that also give rise to latent outcomes. Dewey (1938b) referred to such a phenomenon as collateral learning. He was most concerned about the attitudinal and socialization aspects of learning, including, for example, the development of the desire to learn and the development of certain behaviors and values as they applied to nonschool settings. Dewey saw collateral learning in both positive and negative lights and believed that such learning should not be left to happenstance. Like all curriculum problems, collateral learning had to be consciously conceived of as part of the purposive framework of the curriculum. In other words, the intended curriculum had to be understood in terms of its effects in areas outside the school (use of leisure time, willingness to engage in community service, self-image), areas often assumed to belong in the domain of the family. Jackson (1968) discussed the hidden curriculum in a similar fashion, pointing to the various attitudes learned by students in schools that were related to their ability to function in society (patience, docility, discipline, work roles). The critical theory interest in the hidden curriculum is also tied into these attitudes, but critical theorists seek to identify the political and social significance of these attitudes through an analysis of social control and their "given" view that latent functions of the school curriculum are part of an instrumentality of oppression carried out by the school. There is an underlife to school, they claim, that would go unrevealed and unexamined without the perspectives offered in critical theory.

Much of the psychological literature used to support critical theory perspectives is drawn from Freud and is intended to emancipate the individual through psychoanalysis. Given the supposed instrumental condition of schooling and the relative stress placed on understanding the deep currents that swell beneath the labels and the overall treatment accorded to youth in schools, psychoanalysis is a central resource for critical theory. The surface dimensions of harmony, adjustment, and capitulation, all justified by common-sense reasoning, must be unwrapped to expose their concealed contradictions and malformations, which, more often than not, restrain the individual and the collective group from better understanding and ultimately liberating themselves.

The themes of critical theory are broad ones that exist, albeit with certain embellishments here and there, across radical ranks. There is, of course, diversity within these ranks. Structural Marxists will differ from those who uphold what might be called a humanist Marxist perspective. The broad ideas described above, however, provide a conceptual anchor. The commonalities are substantive, especially as they relate to the interpretation of curriculum history and the belief that the school is an oppressive institution.

CURRICULUM AND THE MORIBUND CONDITION

Critical theory has obviously informed curriculum scholarship through its mission of fundamentally "reconceptualizing" the manner of viewing, analyzing, and interpreting issues of the school curriculum. This effort to reconceptualize the field has had two broad effects.

The first and less prominent effect has been the promotion of alternative pedagogical practices. Pinar and Grumet, for instance, have advocated a phenomenological method of instruction that celebrates individual experience through autobiographical exploration. This method emphasizes the power of the self-encounter, a notion that is quite different from the progressive-experimentalist focus on the collective encounter. Critics such as the Tanners, however, have dismissed the effort to shape school practice through existential phenomenology as an impractical, if not illusory, pursuit. Such initiatives, they claim, often disintegrate into romantic expressions of pursuing one's inner self, leaving educators with unrealistic questions about how to provide an education that asks children to find the meaning of their existence through spontaneous self-realization (Tanner & Tanner, 1980).

The second and main effect generated by reconceptualist views of curriculum has come across as a criticism against what is said to be an encrusted and obsolete view of the curriculum. As the chief spokesperson for this position, Pinar (1978) has claimed that the work of so-called traditionalists in curriculum supports instructional methods that undermine the natural complexity and discordant character of human learning. These traditionalists are said to be driven by a desire to dominate and bring order to a dynamic situation. Curriculum scholars, Pinar argues, would do well to recognize that this perspective is tyrannically behavioristic and anchored in a lineage of thought that attempts to superimpose an industrial mentality on the school curriculum. Moreover, according to Pinar, traditionalists can also be faulted for being too closely bound to the world of the practitioner. Deprived of the needed intellectual distance from the practitioner, traditionalists presumably cannot generate an adequate curriculum theory (Pinar, 1978). Pinar believes this helps to explain why the curriculum literature has been arrested and contains no serious curriculum theorizing.

Reconceptualists are especially critical of using behavioral objectives in the curriculum and reject the general idea of using the curriculum for purposes of planning and management. As will be discussed, behavioral objectives, although they vary in character, are seen as technocratic in nature when they are restricted to observable acts that ignore subjectively experienced human behavior. When this occurs, objectives assume a behavioristic quality that harkens back to the early advocates of activity analysis, who believed that behavioral objectives had to be framed in refined and precise terms. In such circumstances, the curriculum becomes little more than an attempt to bring student behavior into line with normed standards drawn from a multitude of highly specified activities. Interestingly, such a view of curriculum development was criticized with considerable authority by Dewey, Bode, Kilpatrick, and Counts. It should be stressed, however, that behavioral objectives are not necessarily behavioristic, as will be made clear in a later analysis of the Tyler rationale.

In American education, curriculum reform in the public schools has historically been susceptible to sociopolitical forces and swings of emphasis (Cuban, 1990; Goodlad, 1966; Tanner, 1986); at the same time, despite these periodic changes, the schools have been dominated by a behavioristic orientation in instruction (Apple, 1979; Cuban, 1984). The durability of the behaviorist orientation has allegedly resulted in the closing off of vital areas of experience in the classroom and in the reduction of learning to highly mechanical and noncomplex levels (Giroux, 1988b; McNeil, 1988).

Of course, there is a paradox in claiming that intractable and capricious elements coexist in the school curriculum, but, as other scholars have noted, the two conditions are actually two sides of the same coin (Burke, 1978; McKinney & Westbury, 1975). The nature of curriculum reform in America, for instance, does indeed attest to a failure to sustain a substantive direction for the school, an idea that seems to explain the high incidence of cyclicity and educational vogue in school reform formulations. This lack of a steady purposive direction, however, can also be viewed as conducive to the vitality of instrumental features in education, since such features, often touted as neutral and objective in orientation, are purported to have wide applicability. Thus a procedural or instructional approach that can absorb almost any curriculum emphasis or priority will often prevail as a constant amid ostensibly changing periods of reform. Under such circumstances, the "neutral" disposition of behavioristic approaches is favored, and they become prevalent.

Still, the failure of the curriculum field to subdue the apparent faddish character of curriculum change and to have any effect in decreasing the influence of behavioristic perspectives in the school has been analyzed by some as representative of the impoverished quality of curriculum scholarship. Does the curriculum field deserve criticism for failing to temper the flow of reform efforts undertaken without a substantive research base? Has the field contributed to the ahistoricism and reactionary excess that have marked reform initiatives since midcentury? What failings in the field have led to failings in the policy and practice of American schooling?

Several scholars have addressed these questions by describing the historical character of curriculum scholarship as a management construct wedded to solidifying the status quo. The school experience, under such conditions, has suffered under the weight of unquestioned assumptions that have had their origin in bureaucratic thinking and systems procedures. Questions, for instance, about how one should teach have been accepted as extraneous to questions about why some things are taught; efforts to classify youth into instructional categories (tracks and special remedial slots) have been justified as rationally supportable and organizationally necessary; instructional preferences for facts over values and for matching specific behavioristic objectives to performance behaviors have been cast as reasonable ways to organize and direct the school experience. These, to many radical theorists, are the bleak effects of an instrumental rationality that have marginalized the aesthetic and individual experience in the school and have given credibility to the view that curriculum development serves the function of repressive social control.

These allegations have led to a "declaration of moribundity" in so-called established approaches to curriculum theory and development. Interestingly, when this declaration was originally pronounced by Schwab (1970), the problem was attributed not to the predominance of a technocratic rationality but to an overzealous commitment to the prescriptive powers of theory. According to Schwab, the role of theory in curriculum had eclipsed practical concerns, leading to the pursuit of overreaching principles and procedures of curriculum development. The problem lay in the way the theoretical formulations overwhelmed and overlooked the realities of practice. Schwab believed that curriculum theorists had to be diverted from the kind of theoretical pursuits that led to the formulation of universal rules and other invariant instructional elements (e.g., fixed taxonomies and "plug-in" teaching models). Such pursuits, he claimed, though guided by the banner of "theory into practice," were actually ill fitted to practice:

> Theory, by its very character, does not and cannot take account of all the matters which are crucial to questions of what, who, and how to teach; that is, theories cannot be applied, as principles, to the solutions of problems concerning what to do with or for real individuals, small groups, or real institutions located in time and space—the subjects and clients of schooling and schools (Schwab, 1978, p. 287)

Schwab called for the more careful consideration of the practical in the interests of understanding and honoring situational or local conditions. Theory could not act alone in the schooling context; it had to be supplemented by practical arts that kept the real or concrete in focus.

In due time, a similar theme was redeclared by several radical curriculum theorists who went one step further and attached the condition of moribundity to a class of "traditional" curriculum thinkers whose work, by virtue of its effort to apply theory to practice, was purported to be inextricably woven into the fabric of the administrative and managerial prerogative (Pinar, 1978; Pinar & Grumet, 1981). The predominance of the traditionalist group was said to have had a restricting effect on the process of curriculum theorizing as well as on the advancement of the curriculum field itself. In this sense, the "traditionalists" embodied everything that needed to be reformed in curriculum studies; the field had to save itself from itself. And unlike Schwab, who counseled a more intimate association with the practical, the thinking on the Left opted for a more distant theoretical approach (Pinar, 1978).

Not surprisingly, given the talk about moribundity and obsolescence, an adversarial relation developed between those supporting a practical curriculum theory (so-called traditionalists) and those supporting a critical theory. As one might expect, the attitude that the work of traditional curriculum thinkers was in the grip of death and obsolescence did not facilitate the discourse and communication that is often valued in the language of the radical critic. The accompanying charge that traditionalists were doctrinal advocates of social control generated angry reactions that were themselves criticized for failing to cultivate a substantive and advancing discourse (Jackson, 1980; Tanner & Tanner, 1979).

CURRICULUM ORIGINS AND THE MANAGERIAL IMPERATIVE

It is difficult to identify the precise historical moment when curriculum emerged as a systematic area of study. As a specialization, the curriculum field largely arose in the first two decades of the twentieth century, although curriculum considerations had factored prominently into educational theorizing and school program development for many years prior to this period. Different commentators identify different points at which curriculum thought emerged in the educational literature, and they hold very different positions on the legacy of curriculum thinking for schooling.

Pinar and Grumet (1981) equate the birth of the field with the curriculum revision work conducted in the Denver public schools during the 1920s under the direction of Jesse Newlon. Many curriculum scholars have cited Newlon's work as an example of the progressive thinking that led to locally initiated curriculum experimentation and active teacher involvement in school curriculum reform (Kliebard, 1986; Tanner & Tanner, 1980). Pinar and Grumet, however, have described Newlon's influence quite differently. Newlon, they claim, was driven by the desire to put curriculum under the control of the central administrative office in such a way as to subordinate the curriculum to the managerial operations of the school. This, the argument continues, helped set an early management tone for curriculum activity that ultimately led the work of the curriculum field to be consigned to atheoretical service activities—the designing of consensual procedures for school action.

This representation of Newlon as an administrator who used curriculum as a managerial instrument of control goes against the historical record. First, Newlon distinguished himself as a school leader who actually sought to neutralize the effects of managerial utility in the school. Callahan (1962), in his classic study of the business and efficiency forces that shaped the administration of public education, stated that:

> the forceful opposition of educators such as Jesse Newlon and George S. Counts, plus the partial disenchantment with business leadership which accompanied the great depression, helped to reduce the extreme overemphasis upon business and industrial management in educational administration. (p. 248)

Callahan described Newlon as an unusual school administrator, especially for his time, who saw administration as a form of social policy and who, on several occasions, railed against the mechanistic, technocratic nature of the professional priorities of the school administrator. The point is that Newlon not only did not fall prey to the considerable efficiency forces that shaped school administration in his day; he manifestly worked against such forces. In stark contrast to Pinar and Grumet's contention, Cremin observed that Newlon was among the first school administrators to understand and act on the idea of allowing teachers to exercise their own intelligence in the classroom and the school. There was no effort to impose a centralized masterplan of action. In describing the Denver school reform initiated by Newlon, Cremin (1961) stated that:

> The need was not for more committees of administrators, supervisors, and college professors to pronounce on what schools ought to do, but rather for some new device by which teachers themselves could participate in the business of curriculum making. (pp. 299–300)

Newlon did indicate that the school could be used as an instrument of social control, but he cautioned against perverting control to mean loyalty to the status quo and to the nationalistic policies of the state. He spoke directly against autocratic methods of school administration.

> The function and position of the educational administrator is not comparable to that of the employer or the boss in industry. Attempts to draw such a line are pernicious. The administrator does not own the school. Like the teacher, he is a professional worker and a public servant. (Newlon, 1939b, p. 147)

If the idea of curriculum development started with Newlon, its impetus would be more properly characterized as derived from the desire both to liberate teacher intelligence and creativity in the classroom and to assuage the stultifying management procedures roundly practiced by school leaders at the time. Yet, because Newlon sought to bring curriculum thought to the act of school supervision and administration, he is miscast as a voice for social efficiency and for the subordination of the curriculum to central administrative control. Newlon did indeed take an interest in the idea of social control in the curriculum, as will be discussed in a later chapter, but his outlook was appreciably different from the functionalist orientation that often accompanies the doctrine of social control. One begins to see here the double-bind argument that victimizes many liberal-progressives. If Newlon had specifically said that the curriculum should be centrally controlled by administrative designation, he clearly would have been indicted as an advocate of social efficiency and control. Instead, he asserted quite the opposite—but he is nonetheless indicted for latently advancing the interests of administrative control by trying to ally curriculum with school administration. His strongly worded statements against such an outcome are unacknowledged, and their overreached imputation of latent effect is held up as the most meaningful and "real" by-product of Newlon's work. This tautological tactic is used frequently by radical commentators, as we shall see in upcoming chapters.

Not all commentators, including critical theorists, agree that curriculum development was initiated by Newlon as a management activity. Many see Bobbitt's *The Curriculum* (1918) as a more profound influence, one that is also managerial in character; Bobbitt's influence generated an engineering or efficiency model for curriculum development. Kliebard (1975a) has argued that the social-efficiency concerns of the Bobbitt approach have led to a bureaucratic framework for curriculum design and a prevailing factory metaphor for schooling. For Bobbitt, curriculum development was reduced to an itemized list of specific activities (as represented in a composite set of behavioral objectives). Hence the purpose of the curriculum was confined to preparing the learner for specific activities—to teach the learner by direct route in a kind of habit formation process.

The view that places curriculum scholarship in the context of social-efficiency priorities tends to see the legacy of the curriculum field in terms of mastery learning, management by objectives, and other competency-based approaches. Such approaches are precisely the ones that are believed to support a technocratic rationality. Learning, impelled by procedural concerns, is prepackaged as a closed system intended to match behaviors to preordained objectives; the act of curriculum development itself morally neutral, having no egalitarian or other broadly moral purpose. Hence the curriculum becomes merely an instructional delivery program that highlights the implementation of procedures, plug-in models, and other prescriptions that are presumed to be generically applicable, irrespective of the particular characteristics of the classroom and learners. The importance of instructional strategies is justified and made credible through quantifiable measurements that tend to fragment phenomena into an assortment of classifications and labels. In essence, curricularists committed to this line of thought are management specialists who see the curriculum as a grid for prescribing (planning, implementing, and evaluating) learning. They conform to a mentality that seeks to impose universally applicable systems for learning.

Some instructional and curriculum specialists today share this view of curriculum development, supporting such ideas as curriculum mapping, curriculum alignment, direct instruction, time-on-task, and generic teaching strategies (also known as effective teaching strategies). More often than not, these procedural efforts have undermined the organic character of the educational situation, leaving the teacher with a stilted knowledge framework within which to make pedagogical judgments.

Apple (1979) and others have argued further that this preoccupation with efficiency has "depoliticized" the curriculum in ways that tacitly promote established political and economic interests. This failure to see the curriculum in political terms, Apple maintains, has allowed the curriculum to function as a mechanism for the reproduction of the economic, cultural, and class relations in the society—as a mechanism for the production of the technical/administrative knowledge used to exercise social control.

An analysis of curriculum origins, however, is incomplete if it is seen as rooted only in Bobbitt and Charters. As indicated earlier, there was simultaneously a progressive movement that was tied to the experimentalism of Dewey and the pragmatic tradition of cultivating intelligent human action through a method of thinking (reflection through the scientific method). According to the Tanner and Tanner (1980), the seminal bases for curriculum theory are found in Dewey's *The Child and the Curriculum* (1902a) and his landmark *Democracy and Education* (1916).

The view of curriculum informed by Dewey begins with the consideration of the fundamental factors in the educative process, which Dewey identified as the nature of the learner, the values and aims of the society, and the world of knowledge represented in the subject matter. These sources, as Deweyan insights, have had a legacy in the curriculum field, especially among progressive-experimentalists. Tanner and Tanner (1980) have identified a lineage of thought that supports the three factors, including Rugg's (1927) Committee on Curriculum Making, Bode's *Education at the Crossroads* (1938b), the curriculum innovation effort of the Eight-Year Study (Giles, McCutchen, & Zechiel, 1942), Taba's (1945) exposition on the general techniques for curriculum planning, and Tyler's (1949) well-known rationale. These factors point not toward a linear method of curriculum development but toward an orientation to mediate the school experience. In this way, the curriculum is indeed faced with certain circumscribing boundaries, an idea that is inimical to critical theorists.

Curriculum development in this tradition seeks the harmonic interaction of the three factors (learner, society, and subject matter) and is supportive of the scientific method as the governing principle for systematic curriculum construction. To Dewey, the essentials of learning are derivatives of an experimental condition. The reconstruction of knowledge, commitment to reflective thinking for social amelioration, development of a moral purpose moved by reason, effort to empower individuals with the skills to control their own fate, and overarching faith in the enlightening powers of problem-focused inquiry testify to this experimentalist bias. These issues will be taken up again in Chapter 4.

SUMMARY

In recent years, the curriculum field has been faced with a new radical commentary that has touted itself as contributing to a reconceptualization of the field's basic tenets. Many of the criticisms offered by these radical elements have been inspired by a critical theory of education that seeks to slay all commonsense or conventional outlooks. The call for a reconceptualization derives from the belief that curriculum study has historically been associated with an atheoretical management agenda that compresses the school experience into low-level group procedures. There is indeed a facet of curriculum thought that could be characterized in such manner; there is also a distinctive legacy of behavioristic manipulation, generated by this tradition, that continues to prevail in the schools. However, the formal study of curriculum theory and development cannot be reasonably reduced to the laws of efficiency and control that drive business/management strategy. It strains credulity to posit the entire development of the curriculum field in such a manner when the growth of the field paralleled the growth of the progressive movement in education. The voice of the formidable progressive forces, which included individuals such as Dewey, Counts, Rugg, and Bode, was not unheard in or merely incidental to the curriculum field.

Unfortunately, when curriculum history is drawn with a straight ideological line, distortion results and central figures in the field undergo an unjustified revision. While Jesse Newlon, for instance, could be said to have brought the idea of curriculum to the field of administration, he was not, as has been alleged, driven by the desire to put everything under the control of an administratively controlled directorate. In stark contrast, Newlon actually worked to alleviate the central managerial demands of the school by calling for the release of the classroom teacher's intelligence and creativity and by advocating experimentation in the fashioning of learning experiences.

CHAPTER 2

THEORY AS PROTEST

> Curriculum development without curriculum theory is tragic; curriculum theory without curriculum development denies the essential purpose of the theory.
>
> Ralph Tyler

The voice of protest is vital to the health of every scholarly community. It supplies the questions and challenges that set the conditions for inquiry into the beliefs, values, experiences, techniques, and histories of a field. Protest, whether pedagogical or social in character, has long been fundamental to the curriculum literature. Early progressive scholars in American education engaged in their own form of protest by reacting against what was seen as a desiccated form of schooling that stressed mental exercises of rote and recitation. The birth of the curriculum field itself can be partially seen as a reaction against timeworn traditionalist approaches. The value of this protest lay in its challenge to old assumptions and in the path it cleared for new questions and new practical alternatives.

The modern radical critique clearly fulfills the very important function of protest. The force of its argument, especially the manner in which it has highlighted gender, racial, and cultural struggle in public education, has led many in the curriculum field to renegotiate their own positions. However, much of the oppositional thought that radicals have brought to curriculum study is overdrawn and distorted. It attacks traditions of thought with little regard for historical nuance, and, in the end, it creates a criticism based on an *a priori* acceptance of the malevolence of schooling and vaguely constructed proposals for emancipation and existential freedom in the classroom. The result is an ideologically divided world of curriculum discourse that forces a choice between "friend or foe" and between distinctly different views on the form, function, and effects of schooling.

THE SLAYING OF THE TRADITIONALISTS

As indicated, several curriculum theorists have pointed to the need for a reconceptualization of thought in the curriculum field. This argument has been made on the grounds that dominant curriculum thought is wedded to a traditionalist model of schooling that has revealed itself through its allegiance to the Tyler rationale and to the broader belief that all schooling should be preplanned and organized according to behavioral objectives. This attack against traditionalists has been characterized by ideological accusations of obsolescence, ahistoricism, and conceptual myopia (Giroux, 1988b; Pinar, 1978).

Not surprisingly, the protest has failed to achieve much in the way of communication and progress; in fact, given the intemperate quality of the arguments made on both sides of the issues, the more prominent effect of the protest literature seems to have been divisiveness and anger. To understand the problem, one needs to examine the historical interpretations of the curriculum offered by the radical curriculum community. These interpretations are influenced by the very kind of ideological construction of reality that radical thinkers are committed to dismantling.

Categorical Pitfalls

The attack against dominant curriculum thinking is dependent on a categorical treatment of a wide range of curriculum thinkers. For Pinar (1978), the field can be understood as made up of three categories of thinkers: traditionalists, conceptual-empiricists, and reconceptualists. Traditionalists, who are described as wedded to the Tyler rationale and to the atheoretical service of preplanning curriculum procedures in the school, are said to be most popular in the schools. Conceptual-empiricists, who are described as sharing the traditionalist regard for a scientistic rationality, attempt to influence the school experience not so much through planning as through research-sanctioned ideas of generic applicability. Reconceptualists are iconoclasts who wish to liberate the school experience from the positivistic knots of control that are said to be embedded in the ideas of the traditionalists and conceptual-empiricists and to undermine situational learning conditions.

The traditionalists are made up of a broad group of thinkers, none of whom ever judged or labeled their own work as traditional. Pinar (1978) lists Tyler as the most visible and focused traditionalist. Other historical curricularists on his list are Alexander, Doll, Saylor, Shores, Smith, Stanley, Stratemeyer, and Taba; among contemporary curriculum scholars, John McNeil, Zais, and the Tanners are included. This lineage of thinkers is said to adhere to a paradigm of curriculum construction based on a production model of learning and of social engineering.

Among reconceptualists, the categorical treatment of the traditionalists has not been questioned. Giroux (1979), for instance, declared that the curriculum field has been dominated by the technocratic rationality of traditional curriculum theory and design, which "can be found in varied forms in the work of Tyler, Taba, Saylor and Alexander, Beauchamp and others" (p. 249). Elsewhere Giroux (1988b) summarized the assumptions of the traditional curriculum in the following manner:

> (a) Theory in the curriculum field should operate in the interests of lawlike propositions that are empirically tested; (b) the natural sciences provide the "proper" model of explanation for the concepts and techniques of curriculum theory, design, and evaluation; (c) knowledge should be objective and capable of being investigated and described in a neutral fashion; and (d) statements of value are to be "separated" from "facts" and "modes of inquiry" that can and ought to be objective. (p. 13)

Ironically, most of the so-called traditionalists listed above distinguished themselves as progressive reformers in their day. Tyler is the most obvious case. As director of the Eight-Year Study, Tyler helped to assess the curriculum development work conducted in experimental high schools, all of which were united in their desire to reject traditional programs (Tanner & Tanner, 1979). Tyler was clearly far more liberal and less mechanical in his deliberations about curriculum development than any of the proponents of instructional objectives, with whom he is often associated (Eisner, 1979). Even in his famous rationale, which many radicals consider the apotheosis of management thought in curriculum, Tyler displayed a regard for curriculum development that approximated the work of Dewey much more closely that of Bobbitt or Charters, even though Charters was his mentor at the University of Chicago during the early decades of the century.

Fortunately, others have acknowledged the Deweyan influence among more mainstream voices in the field, thus attenuating the validity of the charges against traditionalists. Schubert (1987) observed, for instance, that the authors of major curriculum texts (who have been largely categorized as traditionalists), including Smith, Stanley, and Shores (1957), Taba (1962), and Tanner and Tanner (1980), have:

> Deweyan origins ... that can be seen in their emphasis on diagnosis of situational needs and interests in the context of the classroom, and on the advocacy of scientific and democratic problem-solving as a basis of continuous reconstruction of the curriculum by those who live there, viz., teachers and students. (p. 13).

Moreover, since the curriculum field is perceived to be overwhelmingly comprised of traditionalists (Pinar, 1978), it is also important to note the widespread influence of Dewey among the curriculum professorate. Studies that have identified the most influential or significant works in the curriculum field, as ranked by curriculum professors, testify to the high standing of Dewey's work, not Bobbitt's work (Schubert, Posner, & Schubert, 1982; Shane, 1981). No other thinker has influenced curriculum scholars as profoundly as Dewey.

Many, of course, may question whether Dewey has indeed informed the work of the dominant curriculum perspective. Dewey, after all, is invoked in support of a wide range of positions. Radical theorists might suggest, for instance, that little has actually been learned from Dewey—that his work has endured in the main currents of the curriculum literature only as a rhetorical decoration for what is, in reality, a body of scholarship more closely associated with the social-efficiency influence of Bobbitt. The evidence, however, does not support such a contention. It is true that many traditionalists supported the idea of control in the curriculum, but such an idea was not taken from the engineering focus that radicals like to isolate, but from a carefully crafted notion of progressive self-control formulated by Dewey in *Democracy and Education* (1916) and *Experience and Education* (1938b). The waters, however, run even deeper than this.

A large part of Dewey's influence among curricularists was due to the fact that he broached the idea of connecting curriculum theory and practice with an inquiry or problem-solving process. Dewey (1916) based this problem-solving process on reflection. He believed that genuine experience had to be mediated through a method of thinking or intelligence, and such a method was exemplified in, though not identical with, the scientific method:

> Processes of instruction are unified in the degree in which they center

in the production of good habits of thinking. While we may speak, without error, of the method of thought, the important thing is that thinking is the method of an educative experience. The essentials of method are therefore identical with the essentials of reflection. They are first that the pupil have a genuine situation of experience—that there be a continuous activity in which he is interested for its own sake; secondly, that a genuine problem develop within this situation as a stimulus to thought; third, that he possess the information and make the observations needed to deal with it; fourth, that suggested solutions occur to him which he shall be responsible for developing in an orderly way; fifth, that he have opportunity and occasion to test his ideas by application, to make their meaning clear and to discover for himself their validity. (Dewey, 1916, p. 163).

The idea that a problem-solving method could help govern systematic inquiry in the curriculum became a legacy in the field of curriculum, originally drawn from Dewey's exposition on the nature of method and later used, as Tanner and Tanner (1980) explain, in significant curriculum works, including the work of the Eight-Year Study, Taba's general techniques of curriculum planning, and Tyler's rationale.

Interestingly, when the category of reconceptualization, which Pinar had originally constructed, eventually turned against him in a series of critiques, he acknowledged the problems that categorical treatments generate. The category of reconceptualization implied an adherent status that did not exist among radicals, noted Pinar. The same, however, should have been said about his other categorical treatments, especially the traditionalist category. Such an acknowledgment, however, would have largely neutralized the claims made against the traditionalists and made "the reconceptualization of the field" a less meaningful exercise. Pinar (1980) did later acknowledge that "traditionalists" comprise a "broad thematic territory" that is tied together by an interest in working with practitioners and in using a journalistic writing style. The category of traditionalist, however, was never amended to remove its blanket association with administrative imperatives and with the imposition of axiomatic procedures on the school experience.

The Tyler Rationale Reappraised

In 1970, Kliebard described the Tyler rationale as intellectually sympathetic to Franklin Bobbitt's production model for curriculum development (Kliebard, 1970/1975b). So designed, the rationale was purported to reduce the school curriculum to a product-control function that justified behavioristic and efficiency-driven instruction. Accepting this criticism, other curriculum theorists, most of radical leanings, have argued that the rationale has constricted curriculum thought (Pinar, 1975) and created a rigid concern for production outcomes (proximity to precisely stated ends) at the expense of variant experiential processes (McNeil, 1986). Given these perceived problems, Kliebard's early call to recognize the inadequacy of the rationale as a guide for curriculum development has been echoed by other curriculum thinkers.

Interestingly, the rather striking criticisms lodged against the Tyler rationale have generally gone undebated. Tyler, while acknowledging what he believed to be a misperception of his rationale, never responded substantively either to Kliebard's 1970 reappraisal or to the radical criticism that followed it. Because he saw his rationale as an outline of questions that might be considered in developing a curriculum and because his critics posed no alternative method for studying questions relevant to curriculum planning, Tyler declined to criticize the positions taken against him. Moreover, the message to Tyler from the critics was not always unified. Kliebard (1975b), for instance, flatly asserted that the rationale failed to delineate enough boundaries to be used in deciding what should be included in (and, by implication, excluded from) the curriculum. "The rationale offers little by way of a guide for curriculum making," noted Kliebard, "because it excludes so little" (p. 78). Such a view, however, is difficult to reconcile with the claims of other critics that the rationale uses a controlling, prescriptive language (Huebner, 1975; Pinar, 1975) or that the rationale represents a repressive recipe for curriculum planning (McNeil, 1986).

The view, as originally articulated by Kliebard, that the Tyler rationale is intellectually sympathetic to the curriculum-making techniques of Bobbitt is fundamental to the accusation of educational engineering made against the Tyler rationale. Several curriculum writers have pointed directly at Bobbitt in describing the heritage of curriculum thought from which the Tyler rationale presumably emerged (Apple, 1979; Molnar & Zahorik, 1977; Pinar, 1975). Kliebard (1975b) minced few words in associating the Tyler rationale with behavioral objectives:

> Almost all we have done on the question of the role of objectives in curriculum development since Bobbitt's day is, through some verbal flim-flam, convert Bobbitt's "ability to" into what are called behavioral

> objectives or operational terms and to enshrine the whole process into what is known as the Tyler rationale. (p. 45)

The implication here is not only that the Tyler rationale failed to improve on Bobbitt's work, but that it acted to legitimize the role of behaviorism and narrow specificity in curriculum thinking. Such a criticism maintains that Tyler, like the early advocates of activity analysis, held that curriculum objectives had to be framed as refined and precise behaviors in order to create the conditions for easy quantitative analysis of curriculum effectiveness. According to Kliebard (1986), Tyler believed that "objectives should not be stated in vague terms such as knowing, appreciating and understanding, but in terms that would describe in rather precise terms how the student would behave after a period of study" (p. 220). Furthermore, Kliebard argued (as have several who have followed in his footsteps) that the logic of the Tyler rationale is consistent with the logic of Bobbitt, which posed curriculum as an attempt to match student behavior with normed standards drawn from a multitude of highly specified activities.

This purported linkage of Tyler to Bobbitt, however, is not very profound; on close examination, the two scholars are more dissimilar than similar. Tyler (1949), for instance, argued for a small number of objectives framed at high levels of generalizability. He also advanced mediating considerations (the nature of the learner, the values and aims of society, and the consideration of specialized subject matter) in the pursuit of objectives as a way to protect against the mechanical treatment that marked Bobbitt's approach to curriculum making. In addition, he warned repeatedly against excessive specificity in defining and measuring behavioral objectives, noting that the rationale need not be used in a stepwise or rigidly linear fashion.

The work of Bobbitt, on the other hand, was built on principles of industrial management and its attendant regard for finished products and conveyor-belt processes. Bobbitt (1913) did not express this idea subtly: "Education is a shaping process as much as the manufacture of steel rails" (p. 11). Based on this commitment to the application of manufacturing processes to education, he sought to atomize the curriculum with innumerable objectives derived from major areas of adult experience. Through the method of job or activity analysis, Bobbitt created an itemized list of specific abilities that were presumably needed for successful adult life (areas of occupational performance were particularly important);

he then translated this list into a set of curriculum activities. The intent was to be as specific as possible because the job of the curriculum was to prepare the learner for specific tasks by a direct process of habit formation. As a result, Bobbitt's curriculum was filled with hundreds of skills and behaviors that, by virtue of their specificity, were fixed at a low, mechanical level. Such a mechanistic vision of curriculum was associated with a mechanistic learning psychology; in this respect, the stimulus–response terms of behaviorism provided an amiable theoretical partner (Tanner & Tanner, 1980). Bobbitt posited no mediating factors in determining curriculum objectives. Objectives, to him, were identified by the direct observation and later subdivision of broad categories of human activity (Franklin, 1986). Moreover, to Bobbitt, the very purpose of public education was to foster the growth of the nation's industrial complex, a notion that is not detectable in the work of Tyler.

There are, to be sure, elements in the Tyler rationale that conjure up behavioristic images and can lead to the mistaken impression that Tyler advanced a closed-systems approach to curriculum development. For example, Tyler's (1949) characterization of education as "a process of changing the behavior patterns of people" indeed resembles the connectionist patterns of learning posited by behaviorists (pp. 5–6). Similarly, Tyler's penchant for suggesting that objectives can be drawn out of the relationship between present conditions and desirable norms seems to indicate that learning is a narrow affair that depends on the elimination of ambiguity and variance. Some instructional behaviorists have misused the rationale in precisely this manner. Popham and Baker (1970), for instance, used the rationale to construct a linear curricular system that started with the fragmented consideration of the three sources (the learner, the society, and the subject matter), passed through the processes of formulating and screening general objectives, and concluded with the precise specification of instructional objectives. Such a sequence of activity, however, violated the organic quality of the rationale and offered an ends-versus-means distinction between curriculum and instruction. As will be explained, Tyler warned against such linear and mechanistic applications.

As Reid (1975) has indicated, the main problems attributed to the rationale often have had more to do with the logical extensions that it invited and the essential factors that it omitted, rather than with anything Tyler specifically recommended. Still, to criticize Tyler for what he did not write (and for what others have appropriated) is to perform an injustice against what he *did* write. There is a broad and cautious quality to the rationale that belies the behavioristic characterizations of it.

The issue of specificity and precision in the construction of behavioral objectives, for example, has not been properly represented in criticisms of Tyler. According to Kliebard (1975b), the operational purpose of the rationale is to "state certain design specifications for how we want the learner to behave and then attempt to arrive at the most efficient methods for producing it quickly—and I suppose, cheaply" (pp. 45–46). Unquestionably, Tyler (1949) valued clarity in the specification of behavioral objectives, claiming that desired behaviors must be accompanied by some specification of a particular content or area of life in which the behavior is to operate. It should be emphasized, however, that Tyler did not at any time make these claims in the name of efficiency and cost-saving. Moreover, Tyler discussed at length the dangers of specifying behavioral objectives in terms too precise or too narrow. In fact, he made it absolutely clear that his own bias was to opt for a few objectives that were highly generalizable as modes of thinking and social skills. "Objectives are more than knowledge, skills and habits," he wrote. "They involve modes of thinking, or critical interpretation, emotional reactions, interests and the like" (Tyler, 1949, p. 29). Thus, he continued, "I tend to view objectives as general modes of reaction to be developed rather than highly specific habits to be acquired" (p. 43). To Tyler, the answers to the questions raised in the rationale were dependent on contexts and on a fundamental sense, among school leaders, of a philosophy of life. In this way, Tyler was attentive to local thinking rather than seeking to quash all autonomous thought with a content-neutral management model. When Tyler did refer to efficiency, he spoke of the multiple outcomes resulting from broadly framed, highly generalizable, and logically integrated objectives. Curiously, the distinction that Tyler repeatedly offered between general and specific objectives has not been reflected in the criticisms made against the rationale.

This issue of generalizability is central because it defuses a large part of the argument that describes the Tyler rationale as a systems-management device that imposes an industrial ideology on the public school. If high generalizability is the key, behavioral objectives cannot be viewed as serving a repressive, controlling function; rather, they become fundamental ways of cultivating "generalized modes of attack upon problems" as well as "generalized modes of reaction to generalized types of situations" (Tyler, 1949, p. 42). Such a viewpoint is at odds with the work of Bobbitt. Hence, even if

Tyler and Bobbitt shared a certain logic in framing the relationship between behaviors and norms, the nature of the objectives and the careful effort by Tyler to offer reference or mediating points for their contemplation are indicative of two basically different positions.

After the publication of *Basic Principles of Curriculum and Instruction*, Tyler continued to speak directly to the abuses of specificity in the curriculum. In the midst of the back-to-basics retrenchment of the 1970s, when the conception of learning through the acquisition of specific patterns of behavior again became popular, Tyler (1973) bemoaned the fact that many educators had confused clarity of objectives with specificity and had lost sight of the idea that generalized understanding could be stated clearly and appropriately as objectives. He also claimed that too little thought had been given to the nature of learning and the purposes of education, oversights that were abuses in the rationale. His early distance from Bobbitt was clear when he recalled how his early service studies in higher education were built on the idea that behavior

> Included all kinds of reactions people carry on—thinking, feeling, and acting. . . . I was not using the term as it was used by the school of behaviorism, which restricted it only to overtly observable acts and ruled out much of human behavior that is subjectively experienced but is not directly observable by others. (Tyler, 1973, p. 55)

To posit a kindred spirit between the work of Bobbitt and that of Tyler is simply not a carefully considered analysis. There is a similar logic in the relationship they both posit between objectives and norms. However, Tyler differs from Bobbitt in his explicit interest in providing broad learning experiences rather than learning for specific skill and job performance. There is thus no basis for the accusation that the Tyler rationale is simply an adornment to a legacy of efficiency-driven curriculum procedures.

Few scholars dispute that the three sources identified by Tyler as intervening elements in the consideration of behavioral objectives (studies of the learner, studies of contemporary life, and suggestions about objectives from subject-matter specialists) are rooted in the fundamental factors that Dewey identified as the educative process in *The Child and the Curriculum*. In Dewey's (1902a) words, "The fundamental factors in the educative process are an immature, undeveloped being; and certain social aims, meanings, values incarnate in the mature experiences of the adult" (p. 4). The latter factor is manifested in the specializations and divisions of the bodies of knowledge. Hence Dewey (1902a) cautioned that if the fundamental factors are taken separately and are made into antagonists, a dualism arises between "the importance of the subject-matter of the curriculum as compared with the contents of the child's own experiences" (p. 7).

However, scholars disagree about Tyler's debt to Dewey. Thus, in criticizing the Tyler rationale, Kliebard (1975b) acknowledged the association between Tyler's sources and Dewey's factors; but he made two important distinctions. First, he claimed that Tyler constructed his sources in juxtaposition to one another—unlike Dewey, who saw them in organic unity. Second, he claimed that the consideration of the subject matter was not really a source of objectives but rather a means (an expression of what knowledge is most worthwhile) that arises out of broader sources and influences. These distinctions are important because they helped Kliebard demonstrate that the rationale was linear and fragmented in its treatment of the school experience.

For what were probably analytical purposes, Tyler described the three sources as separate elements. Thus, for example, Tyler (1949) stated that the purpose in studying the learner as a source for educational objectives was to "identify needed changes in behavior patterns of the students which the educational institution should seek to produce" (p. 6). So described, the learner could be perceived as an element to be narrowly manipulated and controlled (much in the tradition of the behaviorists); to Tyler's critics, this seemed to confirm the rationale's role in advancing a systems approach to learning whose purpose was to match student behavior to an itemized list of habits to be formed.

The vitality of such an argument, however, hinges on treating each of the three sources in isolation. To advance a Bobbitt-like curriculum procedure, the norms to which student behaviors are compared would need to be drawn exclusively from one source (society), coupled with a philosophical choice to represent and reproduce the conditions of adult life. In other words, the Bobbitt legacy could only be fulfilled by making the school a place to fit students specifically into the narrow functions of adult life. However, this would violate Tyler's insistence that all three sources be considered together. Not surprisingly, given the propensity to cast Tyler in the image of Bobbitt, the rationale has been criticized for supposedly limiting educational objectives to only one source. As Willis (1975) noted, "Tyler claims that identifying activities of contemporary life is the best way to determine educational objectives" (p. 428). Yet Tyler (1949) cautioned explicitly against using only one source in fashioning behavioral objectives: "No single source of information is adequate to provide a basis for wise and comprehensive decisions about the objectives of the school" (p. 5). Moreover, as discussed below, Tyler thought it important to integrate philosophical and psychological concerns with the three sources in the selection of behavioral objectives.

The role of philosophy in curriculum planning is the point on which Kliebard exposes the neutral quality of the Tyler rationale. Because Tyler left the choice of philosophy open, he is accused of formulating a model for curriculum development that might accommodate any philosophical persuasion. Referring to the rationale, Kliebard (1975b) noted:

> One may express a philosophy that conceives of human beings as instruments of the state and the function of the schools as programming the youth of the nation to react in a fixed manner when appropriate stimuli are presented. As long as we desire a set of objectives consistent with this philosophy (and perhaps make a brief pass at the three sources) we have developed our objectives in line with the Tyler rationale. (p. 78)

Tyler has long described the need for local educators to decide on the fundamental philosophical directions of their schools, and he framed questions in the rationale to avoid dictating to educators how they should be answered. The rationale is meant to be attuned to specific learning conditions in the school and its community, not a way of formulating curriculum development from general data. For Tyler, normative questions can only be answered situationally through the application of local philosophical and psychological views.

However, the neutrality of the rationale is seen by some as the logical consequence of a systems-management design that is concerned only with methodology and certitude of outcomes. As Apple (1979) indicated, systems thought, to which he claims the Tyler rationale is wedded, is a methodology without an identifiable content. "Its conceptual emptiness," Apple maintains, "enables its application in a supposedly 'neutral' manner to a range of problems requiring the precise formulations of goals, procedures and feedback devices" (p. 115).

One reason, however, the rationale cannot be accused of imposing a reductionist, consensual routine on the school is precisely because it is not a neutral methodological device, but rather a method in a psychophilosophical context. In his focus on the practical questions of how to plan a curriculum, Tyler has in mind the application of a frame of reference, not the imposition of universally precise rules. "Curriculum building is not a process based on precise rules," he wrote, "but rather it involves artistic design as well as critical analysis, human judgments, and empirical testing" (Tyler, 1981, p. 24). In the rationale, Tyler described philosophy as an essential screen, but it is actually more like a foundation, since different philosophical persuasions lead inexorably to different ways of treating the questions and the sources.

While the rationale does not stipulate a particular philosophy, it does frame philosophical judgment as a prominent factor in the planning of learning experiences. This is significant because, in seeking to make a place for philosophy in the consideration of the school curriculum, Tyler underscored the fact that schools perform a sociopolitical function. In other words, by stressing the social function of the school as a variable significantly affected by philosophical considerations, Tyler made curriculum workers more conscious of the theory used to frame and justify the school experience. There is indeed a neutrality here, since the decision-making power goes to the educator; but there is also accountability, since the rationale would be used to frame objectives deliberately. The very neutrality of the rationale, in this sense, paradoxically demonstrates that there is no such thing as neutrality in the educational process; it highlights the fact that each institution must develop its own philosophy and that schooling may not be treated in a value-free way, thus making the neutral methodology that characterizes systems thought an abhorrent result in the rationale. Furthermore, in this way the rationale actually helps to discourage repressive tactics in the school curriculum. A repressive school mission such as "programming the youth of the nation to react in a fixed manner when appropriate stimuli are presented" (to use Kliebard's example) could be operationalized using the rationale, but because it would be justified as a deliberate mission sanctioned by the school, it would be open to debate by all parties involved in the conduct of the school, and thus an unlikely result.

Despite its overall neutrality, the rationale does foster particular philosophical concerns by demanding that educators deal with the three fundamental sources mentioned earlier (the learner, the society, and the subject matter). For instance, the purpose of using the knowledge of subject-matter specialists as a curriculum source is explained by Tyler as the desire to know what the specialized subject areas have to contribute to the citizen. This source is suffused with the notion of identifying objectives, drawn from the specialized bodies of knowledge, that suggest ideas, values, and modes of thinking appropriate for civic virtue. Similarly, Tyler's insistence that psychological concerns be weighed and his discussion of the importance of active learning and student interest in learning are also part of a frame of reference that is not neutral at all. Later, Tyler (1966) would admit that initially he did not emphasize these factors sufficiently and that the concept of the learner as active and purposeful is an *a priori* psychophilosophical factor. Still, in the original rationale, Tyler made it clear that in curriculum planning serious attention had to be given to the interests, activities, problems, and concerns of the students in ways that contributed to the progressive ideal of the good person leading a good life. In all of the above ways, the rationale was not a neutral delivery system designed to accommodate a systems methodology.

Those who argue that curriculum development is not normative are likely to be resistant to the Tyler rationale. Unfortunately, many of these curricularists have not made the case, as Tyler did, for a practical theory that can inform and guide the argumentation for and the conduct of schooling. Their tone has been negativistic rather than reforming. To cast the work of Tyler into a management and efficiency category, and to imply that this "traditional" perspective is moribund, is to contradict the ideals of dialogue and conversation that many radical theorists espouse. The idea of the dialectic may well demand the questioning of accepted, commonsense approaches, and the Tyler rationale is an apt target, but the lens employed in examining the rationale too frequently casts a distorted image. The evidence does not support the social-efficiency analysis accorded to Tyler's rationale, although the rhetoric continues to try to do so.

The Curriculum Textbook and the Consensual Procedure

According to Schubert (1986), the most popular texts in the curriculum field have been written by, in chronological order, Caswell and Campbell (1935), Smith, Stanley, and Shores (1957), Doll (1964), Saylor and Alexander (1966), and Tanner and Tanner (1980). There is obviously an overlap between these writers and those whom Pinar criticized as traditional in orientation. Schubert

(1986), however, described these texts as "synoptic" in purpose and structure, meaning that they were comprehensive in the considerations that they brought to the issues of curriculum. Thus, while each text favored a specific philosophical perspective, each also took into account historical, philosophical, and practical responses to the events and diversity in the field.

The synoptic curriculum texts identified by Schubert have also been marked by a vigorous commitment to principles of curriculum development and curriculum design; in fact, as Schubert (1986) indicated, the term *curriculum development* often appeared in the titles of these works. Radical critics have viewed this commitment as inviting the exercise of technocratic rationality in the conduct of the school and as further entrenching normative values for the purpose of social control. Thus Pinar and Grumet (1981) imply that the most widely used curriculum texts were really atheoretical training documents that sought to reduce the school curriculum to a practical grid upon which one could plan low-level procedures of group action and consensus. They were, in this view, little more than adornments to the scientist legacy of Bobbitt's job analysis and Tyler's rationale:

> Classic texts in the traditional mode are: *Fundamentals of Curriculum Development* (Smith, Stanley, & Shores, 1957), *Curriculum Development* (Taba, 1962), and *Curriculum Planning for Modern Schools* (Saylor & Alexander, 1966). They all exhibit this conventional view of curriculum training. Tyler's once thin, economical little book had, by the early 1960s, grown thick with items which a future school administrator responsible for the curriculum might want to know in advance. The management concern with smooth operations, with placating competing involvement groups, remains the consuming interest; it is an interest in knowledge Habermas terms "technical." That is, we want to know possible problems and their solutions in advance in order to control their outcomes. (Pinar & Grumet, 1981, p. 23)

Pinar and Grumet make clear their belief that the instrumentalist priorities of Tyler's rationale were extended through their incorporation into the curriculum texts of the 1960s. Consonant with their historical view of curriculum as a managerial service activity, Pinar and Grumet indict the traditionalist curriculum text as yet another instrument of control and oppression in schooling.

Some of the curriculum texts that followed in the wake of Tyler's rationale, particularly Taba's (1962) *Curriculum Development*, were keenly aligned to the notion of preplanning. In this sense, Pinar's fear that the phenomenological world of the student would be discounted in the curriculum is worth noting. Also, in reference to some of the early curriculum texts, Pinar's general criticisms are well taken; the preoccupation with precisely formed behavioristic objectives in many curriculum texts could and perhaps did lead to school experiences that were unresponsive to the changing and emergent character of the educational situation. However, as a group, these so-called traditionalist texts cannot be roundly indicted. Tanner and Tanner's (1980) *Curriculum Development,* for example, attacked linearity and prescriptive approaches in learning and teaching. The Tanners' text not only did not reflect the design specificity that marked the work of the Taba and Alexander–Saylor texts, but argued that such approaches were dangerously narrow.

This blanket condemnation and failure to perceive nuance results in various fictions about the nature of curriculum thought as expressed in the major curriculum texts. The Smith, Stanley, and Shores (1957) text, for instance, advises using all three sources (the learner, the society, the subject matter) in making curriculum formulations and stresses that learning should grow out of the needs of society. It presents a framework for a curriculum based on the development of critical thinking and social insight (Tanner & Tanner, 1979, p. 12). Schubert (1986), in fact, noted that this text supported social reconstructionist themes that stressed social problem solving and student interest in an integrated or interdisciplinary subject format. Even Huebner (1976), a scholar very much informed by critical theory and Habermas's view of technical knowledge, qualified the association between the Smith, Stanley, and Shores text and the behavioristic nature of Bobbitt's work. "Ignored in Bobbitt's analysis," Huebner observed, "but present in that of Smith, Stanley and Shores, is the problem of how culture, in its various manifestations, evolves and changes" (p. 164). Huebner's distinction underscores the fact that the Smith, Stanley, and Shores text cannot be dismissed as a sterile, technocratic effort to restrict school experience to the service cultural consensus and social control.

Yet this text was indeed driven by an effort to scientifically validate the curriculum through precisely articulated behavioral objectives. The text, for example, noted that "objectives must be capable of reduction to behavioristic terms," suggesting a measure of the specificity and atomization that Tyler clearly rejected. It also suggested that Bobbitt's job analysis theory of curriculum construction, if used as "a theory of curriculum determination, not a statement of the methodology of teaching," was still a viable curriculum development strategy (p. 613). Smith, Stanley, and Shores contended, for instance, that the by-products of job analysis were not necessarily mechanistic and narrowly utilitarian—so long as job analysis as a theory could be made responsive to organic conceptions of learning as well as to spiritual and cultural values. This was in effect a redefinition of job analysis that highlighted an understanding of the inherent problems of social predestination, narrow utilitarianism, and curriculum fragmentation in Bobbitt's original idea.

In the final analysis, the Smith, Stanley, and Shores text endorsed an eclectic approach to curriculum development by mixing social reconstructionist elements with behavioristic elements. The text was marked not by ardent advocacy for a point of view, though there clearly was one, but by panoramic descriptions of curriculum development possibilities. In this sense, the text presented points of view on curriculum development that cannot be legitimately described as purely instrumental. The problem with the radical interpretation of the Smith, Stanley, and Shores text is that it latches onto only the behaviorist element and fails to represent the broader elements in the text.

Taba's (1962) text focused much more deliberately on the practice of curriculum development, although it also reflected the Tyler tradition of diagnosing problems in the educational situation and treating them as building blocks for the organization, implementation, and evaluation of the curriculum. Taba has been described by Franklin (1986) as the intellectual heir of Bobbitt, but she is better described as leaning toward the progressive-experimentalist focus captured in the Tyler rationale.

In examining her text, we again encounter the issue of behavioral objectives. Taba (1962) emphasized the principles of clarity and specificity in formulating curriculum objectives, which gives some support to Pinar's contention that this text was influenced by tenets of managerial imposition. She also discussed the need for human engineering in the process of curriculum change, calling for a strategy of modifying attitudes, controlling human behaviors and building curriculum work teams. But Taba's five hundred page text also called for teacher involvement in the diagnosis of curriculum problems and the formulation of curriculum experimentation. She did not wish to limit the school curriculum to a pre-packaged prescription of what was appropriate for the education of children; rather she hoped that teachers would take the risk, through professional deliberation and reflection, of developing the curriculum with a problem-focused strategy that stressed three significant mediating factors: the learner, the society, and the subject matter.

There is a clear linearity in Taba's view of curriculum design as well as a great deal of value placed on preplanning the problems and the subject to be studied in the curriculum. Such priorities can result in a type of oppression, since the curriculum may therefore fail to be attuned to "the end in view," to use Dewey's term, and to the notion that the curriculum must change and grow as children change and grow. To Dewey, the ends of the curriculum were projected actions in the life experience, not separate states; they are evaluated by the concrete means used to achieve them. This means that the relation between the ends and means has to be set in the context of back-and-forth reflection; it cannot be predetermined and set in stone. But since Taba offered so many elements for consideration in the formation of the curriculum and stressed the need for teachers to exercise their own intelligence, she seems to have understood this. Those who engage in curriculum development, Taba (1962) observed, "need to examine unwelcome alternatives, question the merits of cherished teaching procedures as means of achieving objectives, assess relevance of cherished facts as useful knowledge and so on" (p. 463). Moreover, she added, teachers need to be convinced that curriculum revision is dependent not on the wisdom of the "experts" who suggest materials and procedures, but on the ability of teachers to understand their own educational situation. Recognizing this priority in Taba is no less important than recognizing the value that she placed on behavioral objectives. This broader recognition contradicts Pinar's belief that traditionalists such as Taba were moved by a managerial compulsion to "placate involvement groups" and to establish "predesigned procedures of consensus."

THE IDEOLOGY OF PROTEST

According to the radical argument, the neutrality or objective nature of curriculum development and its purported regard for finding the most efficient method eliminate the need to deal with the question of whose knowledge is privileged in the school (and with what sociological effects). The so-called neutrality of curricular judgments is said to be shaped by empirical analytic frameworks of rationality that are presumed to be verifiably valid and fair.

To the radical critic, however, those who claim neutrality in their judgments are not only mythologizing their claims but also misunderstanding an essential principle of school analysis, which is that all rationalizations are ideologically based constructions that stress certain values in ways that favor some groups more than others. The patronage shown to certain groups at the expense of others is the starting point of the argument of oppression and injustice. In the schools, these social constructions are seen as common sense and become natural to the daily ebb and flow of school life, thereby veiling the true ideological impulse of the school. If the ideological themes in the formulations of the school remain hidden, the curriculum will always act to sustain the structural bases of inequality in the society. Likewise, educators and other well-intentioned school personnel will unwittingly contribute to the maintenance of these structural bases. In Apple's (1981) words, "purposeful reasoning and well-intentioned actors . . . may be serving ideological functions at the same moment that they are seeking to alleviate some of the problems facing individual students and others" (p. 134). Thus it is incumbent on school analysts to examine "the patterns of the kinds of individuals who get ahead and the latent outcomes of the institution. These larger social patterns and outcomes may tell us much about how the school functions in reproduction" (p. 135). Concerned with unmasking the dynamics of oppression, injustice, and power in the school, the curriculum theorist seeks to reveal an underlife to schooling that is logically justified and explained but is ultimately marked by some level of malevolence toward marginalized groups.

The Manifest Versus the Latent

As indicated, the concern with the hidden curriculum is of great importance to the radical argument. Through its inculcation of values, its training in behaviors of subservience, and its slotting of students into disempowering categories, the hidden curriculum is believed to reproduce social-class structures and to minister to capitalist interest. The hidden curriculum is, in essence, perceived as an instrument of social control, even though no explicit claim for social control is articulated (Vallance, 1973).

The fact that the hidden curriculum is not acknowledged as a mechanism for social control, however, is believed to be essential to its perpetuation. Educators who unknowingly conduct the hidden curriculum are convinced, through empirical–analytic paradigms of justification, that their manifest efforts in the classroom are supported by rationalist conventions about teaching. Since these manifest efforts have manifest effects (acquisition of skill and knowledge), the hidden curriculum is overshadowed by school actions that have publicly stated rationales (standardized test achievement, mastery of learning objectives, coverage of the "curriculum"). Thus attention is diverted from the latent effects of the hidden curriculum, making it extraneous and ultimately irrelevant to normative concerns.

Radical commentators have attempted to bring the hidden curriculum out of the darkness with a zeal that has actually begun to confuse the relation between manifest and latent functions. As Jackson (1977) observed, in some cases the rhetoric about the hidden curriculum leads to the assumption that "the latent is the real and the manifest is the unreal." In other words, the manifest intentions of schooling (however noble) are sometimes not taken very seriously by radicals because such intentions are believed to cloak the "real" school operations. Thus radical curriculum theorists often see the manifest as potentially less significant and perhaps less relevant than what it is supposedly covering up. In such a scenario, latent functions (e.g., inculcating passivity in poor and minority youth) are taken to be the real ones and manifest functions (e.g., offering enhanced resources and learning opportunities to these youth) are passed over as less significant, as not carrying the "real meaning."

This leads to a serious problem because by ignoring the potential manifest effects of schooling, radical curriculum theorists fail to give proper weight to conserving agendas in the school (the transmission of communicative competence, cultural patterns, and political realities), thereby increasing the potential of relativizing culture in a manner that leaves the school susceptible to romantic and anarchic forces (Bowers, 1984). Barrow (1976) put it another way:

> It may be true that school curricula tend to embody a particular cultural stance but it sometimes seems to be forgotten that for better or worse that cultural stance is the one also embodied in the backgrounds of a great many children. If the argument were simply that the individual's cultural background should be taken seriously and provide the basis of the curriculum, the conclusion would seem inescapable that we would need to reject a common system of schooling. (p. 64)

As will be discussed in the concluding chapter, the disintegration of a common system of schooling is among the more notable effects

of the protest literature, an effect that is promoted, quite paradoxically, by economic conservatives as well.

Dewey (1916) understood the balance required between the
conserving and liberating purposes of the school. He stated the
problem clearly by noting that society exists by transmission as well
as in transmission and that the school, as an engine for the correction of the society, should use the common and shared experience
for selective transmissive purposes as well as for cultivating the social discourse and sense of community so essential to transformative purposes. In this sense, the idea of diversity was seen as an
essential part of the school's common base. It should be noted that
Bowers (1987) has also accused Dewey of failing to deal with conserving agendas in education, noting his failure to place any limits
on what can be viewed as problematic and criticizing his narrow
belief that change, as executed through experimental inquiry, is always desirable. Dewey's apparent sin was his willingness to leave all
cultural canons open to reconstruction. Bowers's point, however,
has to be weighed against Dewey's clear belief in structuring school
experiences along common lines for the purpose of enhancing
the consensual powers of communication and community in the
school. The problem-focused inquiry stressed by Dewey does not
inevitably lead to change and modification. The so-called results of
inquiry can, in fact, be used in support of conserving actions. For
Dewey, inquiry is guided by the values of the society, which itself
represents a conserving principle, and by a process of social mutuality that protects democratic culture from ossification and tyranny.
Conserving possibilities are not extinguished in this context because
all inquiry is regulated by a scientific outlook that can provide evidence against change. Ironically, this is the very position that moved
various historical revisionists to categorize Dewey as a voice for the
status quo. Thus, in regard to the conserving agenda of schooling,
Dewey is in clear contradistinction to the radical position, which
typically views the transmissive purposes of the school as evil, as an
instrument of cultural coercion.

In essence, radical curriculum theorists posit a dualism between the ideals of transmission and those of transformation, not
unlike the dualism that Dewey responded against when the develop-
mentalists of his day sought to promote individualistic endeavors
in the curriculum while conservative humanists aimed to immerse
all youth in the literary traditions of Western civilization (Kliebard,
1986). Such a dualism has had the effect of splitting the scholarly
community into "party-line" allegiances of ideology, or what Bowers
(1991a) calls the friend–enemy relation.

There is, of course, a need to examine both manifest and latent practices in the school curriculum, but the manifest cannot be underestimated. This seems to be understood when the manifest is overtly repressive. Confusion, however, prevails when speculations begin about the latent role of the school curriculum. Such confusion has led to several tautologies in the radicals' assertions of social control and oppression. For example, on the one hand, where middle-class values have been imposed by the school curriculum, minority youth have been said to be disempowered by such stultifying measures; on the other, where middle-class values have been withheld, minority youth have been said to be disempowered by the failure of the school to commit to egalitarian measures. On the one hand, student resistance to the "cultural hegemony" of the school has been interpreted as leading to disabling behaviors because of its association with dropping out of school (mentally or physically); on the other, lack of such student resistance has been interpreted as leading to the disabling behaviors associated with becoming an uninformed conformist. These conflicting generalizations seem to be the result of an overt ideological spinning of the data—the intention of proving a contention (in this case, the contention that schools are oppressive institutions) rather than testing a contention. The irony is that while radical curriculum theory seeks to unravel the ideological wrapping of reality, in doing so it generates its own ideological wrapping. Thus one bias is exchanged for another and the field is taken headlong into an ideological war over the truth.

The Marxist preoccupation with a "monistic theory of social causation," to use Dewey's (1939, p. 72) words, is indicative of the limits of ideology. Ravitch (1977) noted this phenomenon in her criticism of Gintis and Bowles' *Schooling in Capitalist America* (1976):

> Events of the past are shown either to correspond to capitalist imperatives or to be contradictions generated by capitalism. School reforms that took root were a sham because they bolstered the capitalist system, and school reforms that failed were rejected because they threatened the capitalist system. The argument is not susceptible to disproof: The schools don't promote equality or personal liberation because the capitalist system won't let them, but when they do, it is in order to delude the people and serve capitalism. Both A and not-A are advanced as evidence for the same point. (pp. 146–147)

All radicals, of course, cannot be indicted as ideologues, but a good part of their work proposes similar conclusions in the face of conflicting data, all of which supports the idea of an ideological commitment to framing the school as a fundamentally unjust agency. As Gutmann (1987) noted, if one assumes that all educational policies that do not overthrow capitalism are instrumental in its sustenance, virtually any policy emerges as functionally oppressive.

Ideological Determinism

As indicated, radical critics have long maintained that a correspondence exists between the economic structure of the society, which is viewed as being inherently unequal and unfair, and the social institutions of the society. As also discussed, the public school system, despite its rhetorical claims, is believed to be a fundamental part of this equation; it is believed to cultivate the social relations and fundamental dispositions needed to effect the reproduction of the capitalist status quo.

Several Marxist commentators have conceded that such a view may be overly deterministic, failing to account for the diversities and complexities of situational school initiatives, but the message that schools act against the interest of the commonweal and in the interest of capitalism continues to prevail. Giroux (1980) and Apple (1981), for instance, have made it clear that the structuralist analysis offered by reproduction theory is inadequate; it is not nearly sensitive enough to situational messages, values, and norms. Apple (1981) has spoken to the need for educational research to target local factors and to identify the layers of mediation that exist between the economic sector of the society and its other institutions, particularly, in this case, the school. This is a welcome call because, at one level, it acknowledges the possibility that the relation between the school and the corporate society has yet to be understood, and that the fundamental belief that schools actualize the imperatives of the capitalist machinery is at least questionable. Yet most writers informed by critical theory, including Apple and Giroux, continued to assert that schools structurally reinforce the power of dominant groups by exercising economic and cultural hegemony over marginalized ones. Advocacy for this position by radical commentators seems to have been unaffected by the recognized overemphasis on the idea of domination and reproduction. Not only is the reproduction construct still central to the argumentation, but the argumentation itself is marked by an advocacy for the ideological view of reproduction. In Giroux's (1983b) words:

Radical educators have argued that the main functions of schools are the reproduction of the dominant ideology, its forms of knowledge and the distribution of skills needed to reproduce the social division of labor. In the radical perspective, schools as institutions could only be understood through an analysis of their relationship to the state and the economy. In this view, the deep structure or underlying significance of schooling could only be revealed through analyzing how schools functioned as agencies of social and cultural reproduction— that is, how they legitimated capitalist rationality and sustained cultural reproduction. (pp. 257–258)

It is no accident that the issue described by Giroux deals with *how* schools legitimize capitalist rationality, not *whether* they do so. The latter concern is unproblematic to the ideology. Even when concerns are raised about the deterministic flavor of reproduction theory, the issue does not become whether the conclusions may be wrong, but whether there is enough room for "human agency" and the hope for reform and change (Giroux, 1981).

As indicated by Pinar and Bowers (1992), the concept of reproduction has slowly fallen out of grace in the radical critique; that critique now favors the concept of resistance, which looks to the events that contradict and defy the domination of capitalistic interest in the school. The problem, however, is that even the notion of resistance is framed in a manner that accepts the main tenets of reproduction theory; otherwise there would be little to resist. This leads to argumentation that gets caught in a dichotomous treatment of resistance and reproduction. For instance, educators who pass the litmus test for radical pedagogy engage in resistance, using strategies in the classroom that, among other things, interrogate cultural conventions, search for self-meanings, and reflect on the acts of oppression committed against various groups. The absence of such an outlook among educators, however, amounts to complicity in the operationalization of cultural and economic reproduction.

Over the years, much research has been conducted on questions dealing with issues of inequality in schooling as they relate to racial, class, and gender differences. The indictment of the school for reflecting and solidifying these differences has been impressive; but the radicals have been unable to make their case on a systemic or structural level. That is, local initiatives and determinations are essential factors in judging oppression and inequality; it is virtually impossible to draw any general conclusions about what is happening in all the classrooms of American schools. Irrespective of the external forces seeking to influence their behavior (testing, textbooks, supervisory practices, certification priorities), teachers still have the opportunity to exercise their own creativity and intelligence in the classroom. They may default on this opportunity, but in the end, teachers are the final adjudicators of what is taught and how it is taught. Despite "surveillance" systems such as testing, there is indeed evidence indicating that the character of the classroom experience is widely different, a result of the unique dynamism of elements brought to bear in each school and classroom (Pauley, 1991).

Despite the difficulty in drawing broad conclusions about schooling, the radical commentary is nevertheless framed in terms of comprehensive and pervasive levels of school organization. The critique is ideological and is expressed in language that itself helps to establish the radical identity. As Bowers (1991a) observed, phrases such as *social transformation, resistance,* and *emancipatory power* are decontextualized and framed as belonging exclusively to the province of the critical pedagogue. *Emancipation* sounds honorable, but when contextualized it can belong to fascists, fundamentalists, moderates, progressives, and radicals alike. It is not emancipation per se that vibrates as an insight to the radical; it is a kind of emancipation that is wedded to an *a priori* belief in the existence of certain malignancies in the American school. Thus, having made the school inevitably ideological and fundamentally unjust, radical commentators can insist on the primacy of their own methods and concepts (Pinar & Bowers, 1992).

This leads us straight into the friend–enemy distinction that seems to mark radical discourse. The facing off of counterpositions in an atmosphere of hostility is not new to scholarship and is not, of course, particular to the radical critic. The divisive nature of the curriculum field cannot be blamed on the strident rhetoric of radical theorists, although, as mentioned earlier, it has contributed to this problem. What is interesting to note is that the idea of conversation and idea of the dialectic are espoused as central tenets of the radical discourse. Yet the level of incivility in the language of radical theorists is remarkable. Explosive language is often volleyed against views not in conformity with the assumptions discussed earlier. Friendly voices are "emancipating," "liberating," "empowering," and "enabling"; unfriendly voices are "vulgar," "crude," "hegemonic," "disabling," and "disempowering" (Bowers, 1991a, p. 240). The idea of conversation is caressed in the rhetoric of the radical, but the language often offers pain.

In the end, it is important to note that the analysis used by radicals in explaining or unveiling school phenomena as class ideology is itself colored by an ideological intent that generates its own veil and its own unbalanced view of public schooling. Substantive issues of how schools *might* work, according to the highest ideals of the society, are typically eschewed, and the more comfortable issue of explaining how schools do *not* work is embraced. This bias also taints the historical perspective on the curriculum because it leads to the failure to recognize the pragmatic curriculum literature. Much of the work done by Dewey, Rugg, Newlon, Tyler, Kilpatrick, and many others dealt directly with possibilities in the curriculum, complete with actual proposals that spoke to issues of pedagogical craft and school design. These scholars, however, have typically been ignored or wrongfully criticized as driven by an instrumentalist mentality.

A voice built on dissent, disapprobation, and consuming negativity is rarely able to supply its own plan for the construction of educative environments. As mentioned earlier, such a plan would be construed as in "bad faith." Thus radical or critical educational theorists, in their deep and abiding commitment to exposing oppression, disregard the practical question of how to use the heritage of curriculum thought to mitigate the very conditions they stand against.

SUMMARY

The reconceptualist movement in curriculum has been framed as arising from the decline or fall of a dominant traditional curriculum perspective. This traditional view has been characterized as a seamless fabric of thought and action that is historically indebted to early behavioristic and management principles of curriculum development. In truth, much of the so-called traditionalist work is better characterized as emerging out of the pragmatic-experimentalism of John Dewey. The most glaring and significant example of this is the Tyler rationale, which continues to be battered by radical critics as the representative statement on how to delimit the school through efficiency concerns. Tyler's rationale, cognizant of the need to draw boundaries in a school, identifies several factors that have a solid basis in the progressive curriculum literature and organizes them in a manner that might be used to mediate the school curriculum. Its orientation arises out of meliorist beliefs and practices, not social-efficiency ones. Similarly, many of the most popular curriculum texts, which also have been said to be wedded to the notion of prefashioning a repressive recipe for the school, have also, despite being somewhat compromised by behavioristic concerns, taken much from Dewey and other progressives with meliorist leanings. Such historical interpretations seem to have more to do with ideological loading than with open investigation. The deterministic quality of the ideological argument has accepted certain facets of schools as unproblematic and has resulted in precisely the kind of divisiveness in scholarship that Dewey warned against so long ago. In the final analysis, radical commentators have written much about how schools fail to abide by a visionary and enlightened ideal, but they have also left us with little in the way of solutions that might work within the social and political realities of our schools.

CHAPTER 3

CURRICULUM DIRECTION AND THE PROBLEM OF CONTROL

> All learning, whether in or out of school, has to do with the transformation of experience in the interests of better control. In order to bring about this transformation, it is necessary to do something that will produce the desired change.
>
> Boyd Bode

A prevailing theme in the curriculum literature today is the belief that rationalizations of the school curriculum are historically born of the ideological act of social control (Apple, 1979; Franklin, 1986). Bobbitt and Charters are cited as early examples of how educational objectives rested on the bed of cultural consensus and the attendant desire to cultivate an industrial (capitalist) society. As discussed in Chapter 2, several efforts have been made to place Tyler and other "traditionalists" into the same frame of reference.

Among the more troubling by-products of this thesis is the implication that all practical theory in the curriculum is an attempt to eliminate or delimit the dynamic dimensions of the school experience. Increasingly one finds, for instance, that even the desire to convert theory into practice is perceived as yet another way to stress managerial values in the school curriculum in ways that overpower the lived quality of experience (Pinar & Grumet, 1981). According to this position, the conversion of theory into practice amounts to little more than a scheme to implement a preordained set of behaviors that constrict the thinking and the action of students and teachers. As a result, it is believed that, to better serve the curriculum, more distance must be created between theorists and practitioners; theory into practice too often means certitude of outcomes and a stifling anticipatory direction, both of which work against the liberatory and existential needs of practitioners and students.

However, the growing penchant to classify practically any ef-

forts to use the curriculum for purposes of social cohesion and ordered direction as acts of repression and control fails to acknowledge important nuances in the positions of the thinkers implicated
by such a criticism. This failure results in grouping an altogether
eclectic assemblage of curriculum thinkers (including Bobbitt, Caswell, Newlon, Dewey, Tyler, and Taba) into one line of functionalist
thought.

The act of anticipating the direction and outcomes of a school
mission is not an altogether atheoretical or stultifying endeavor. The
Deweyan tradition of casting aims as means (theory into practice)
and of using aims as the projected consequences of action is noteworthy in this respect. Dewey (1916) battled the doctrine of fixed,
external ends by making it clear that means and ends were two ways
of regarding the same actuality; an aim had to grow up within an
activity as a plan for its direction. Aims had to be translated into a
method of cooperation and organization in the school curriculum.
"An aim," declared Dewey (1916), "implies an orderly and ordered
activity, one in which the order consists in the progressive complet-
ing of a process" (p. 102). Therefore, the translation of theory into
practice and the effort to achieve a sense of order in the framing of
a deliberately conceived educative environment are not inherently
inimical to the learning and teaching experience; rather they are
fundamental ways of accepting responsibility for the achievement
of an aim. This is not merely a procedural position; it is a theory of
conduct that strives to redirect action as it emerges from action.
There is a quest for a kind of control, but it is never final and closed
and is always in process, leaving the learner with a consciously directed and purposeful quality of experience. As Dewey (1916) observed, control need not be coercive and compulsive: "Control, in
truth, means only an emphatic form of direction of powers, and
covers the regulation gained by an individual through his own efforts quite as much as that brought about when others take the
lead" (p. 24). In fact, control factors always prevail in the context of
learning. As Dewey (1916) noted, "internal control through identity
of interest and understanding is the business of education" (pp. 39–
40); the question is not whether or not there will be control but
what its nature will be.

Dewey underscored the point that control accrues as a consequence of the best management of present means and problems.
One can never know ahead of time the amount or the specific nature
of control, because to prefashion it and make it a direct aim would
be to misuse its central function of directing emergent problematic

situations. "Control of the future," Dewey stated (1922), "is indeed precious in exact proportion to its difficulty, its moderate degree of attainability" (p. 266).

CURRICULUM CONTROL AND THE BEHAVIORISTIC LEGACY

The origin of the behavioristic perspective in curriculum could well be traced to Bobbitt and his development of the curriculum-making technique called job analysis. The technique was indeed behavioristic in orientation, meaning that it was influenced by a closed-systems theory that called for a mechanistic approach to curriculum construction influenced by a connectionist psychology of learning. Behavioristic approaches to curriculum are also influenced by the assumptions of logical positivism, which holds that knowledge is best generated by empirical–analytic rules anchored in the instrumental method of science. Positivism is openly committed to the "objective and value-free" world of facts and operates in the interests of efficiency. Even for its advocates, positivism, when applied to curriculum development, is circumscribed by the belief that one must deal with facts; that means and ends are separate (and clearly formulated); that school solutions should be based on empirical data; and that the curriculum is a logically planned intervention that can work effectively to attain preformulated ends (English, 1983).

Behavioristic prejudices have, over the past several decades, helped to sanction reductionist models of instruction in the schools, including such innovations as competency-based instruction, mastery learning systems, teacher-proof materials, performance contracting, accountability testing, and programmed instruction. These attempts to apply formulaic approaches to teaching have contradicted the complex nature of classroom teaching by reducing the teacher's role in curriculum to its most rudimentary and routine elements. As a result, teachers continue to be described as suffering from a narrow technician mentality. According to Giroux (1988b), the problem is systemic to the school, where a traditional pedagogy of narrow standardization aims only to transmit knowledge uncritically to students, thereby placing the teacher in the unimaginative position of imparting the information and skills predetermined as most worthwhile. As McNeil (1988) indicated, there are school districts today that seek to take both the choice of curriculum elements and the means of testing students away from teachers and place them in the hands of external agents looking to redesign the curriculum for the purpose of bringing it into alignment with the material used on standardized exams. This results in an engineering approach to teaching and learning in which the teacher's influence in essential areas of pedagogy and curriculum development is at least weakened, if not entirely usurped. Rather than searching for improvements to established practices, the teacher is told to focus on the mechanics of instruction to the exclusion of content decisions.

Behavioristic influences have also helped to foster the current instructional preoccupation with lower intellectual processes and the accompanying disproportionate regard for the isolated development of basic facts and skills. Today there still seems to be a general failure to see the connection between the subject matter and relevant personal and social concerns; instead there is often a highly discipline-centered treatment of the subject matter, with the teacher's goal being simple fact accumulation and subject mastery. The subject matter itself, often organized in the most abstract and puristic terms, becomes the curriculum; maneuvering through it with effective instructional procedures becomes the teacher's main concern. The result is similar to what Friere (1973) called "banking education," a condition whereby teacher narration provides students with academic content (foreign to the needs of the learner and the society) that students uncritically receive, memorize, and repeat. Goodlad's (1984) national study of American schooling provided some support for the existence of banking education. Goodlad found, for instance, that in many subject areas, the teaching techniques had a narrative and mechanical character that was driven by the desire to "deposit" a disparate accumulation of facts and generalizations into the students' heads. In the teaching of social studies, for instance, most classroom activity centered on memorization of facts; in language arts, the focus was on the mechanics of word recognition, phonics, vocabulary development, and the basics of grammar. Across all subject areas, Goodlad found that a rather traditional lecture format, pitched to a low level of intellectual challenge, was standard operating procedure. And when the teacher was not lecturing, Goodlad found that students busied themselves with relatively narrow and unsophisticated levels of individual seatwork. Clearly, the instructional preoccupation of the behavioristic tradition is amenable to the functionalist purpose of acquiring the academic knowledge and the "shared" cultural values and beliefs inherent in a conservative-humanist agenda (Bennett, 1987; Hirsch, 1987); thus strict instructional tactics can be construed as tools for control because they fail to challenge the content of what is being taught.

The research literature in this tradition has also upheld a repressive notion of control by supplying the profession with ideas that have kept teachers from developing a more expansive curriculum vision and intelligence. One of the more recent major ideas emerging from this literature, for instance, is the principle of time-on-task (which espouses the unremarkable conclusion that learners should be engaged in classroom activities). It is obvious that engagement is a prerequisite for learning, but all forms of engagement are not educative. Since the time-on-task dictum does nothing to underscore the qualitative character of the task, it can legitimately be seen as an idea justified by technocratic concerns. Among school professionals, especially teacher supervisors, time-on-task has been interpreted to mean that good teaching is marked by high levels of engagement, irrespective of the nature of the learning engagement. Thus the notion of time-on-task has little worth unless an effort is made to systematically evaluate the relative quality of the classroom tasks.

The effective-teaching literature is another example of the short-sightedness of purely instructional knowledge. Shulman has argued that the empirical research on effective teaching has oversimplified the teaching situation by dwelling on managerial forms of instruction. According to Shulman (1987), critical features of teaching—such as the subject matter being taught, the classroom context, the physical and psychological characteristics of students, and the accomplishment of purpose not readily assessed on standardized tests—are typically ignored in the quest for general principles of effective teaching. Indeed, the assumption is that "effective teaching" is removed from such considerations.

Not surprisingly, the educational literature has also been overridden by the popularity of strictly instructional models to school and staff development. The popular Hunter approach is perhaps best known. The Hunter approach lists various structural elements of a lesson (anticipatory set, statement of objectives, careful monitoring for understanding, guided and independent practice, and a sense of closure) as the foundation of effective pedagogy. Since the early 1980s, it has dominated teacher inservice programs throughout the nation, affecting the thinking and behavior of thousands of teachers. Some school districts have even used the Hunter approach as the main criterion by which to judge teacher aptitude and thereby made it a factor in promotion and salary decisions. Slavin

(1987) maintained that the Hunter model has taken on the quality of a panacea, with many school administrators thinking that they cannot do without it. Purely as an instructional model, however, the Hunter model is far from holding the key to good teaching. According to Anderson (1988), the Hunter model may be usefully used with some learners in some situations, but overall "it suffers from a highly directive orientation in which there is only one definition of 'good' teaching" (p. 77). Teachers may successfully execute the model; but the question of how teachers should proceed from the standpoint of instruction is without merit unless it is jointly framed with the questions of what is being taught, why is it being taught, who is being taught, and how can it be better taught in subsequent interactions. To embrace a single model as a closed and complete instructional system is to generate an educational myopia that does little to advance the vitality and variety of the school experience. In fact, it comes dangerously close to reducing the act of teaching to formulaic and routine patterns. As Dewey (1916) stated, "nothing has brought pedagogical theory into greater disrepute than the belief that it is identified with the handing out of teachers recipes and models to be followed in teaching" (p. 170).

So-called instructional specialists are not the only ones who have attempted to separate the realm of curriculum from the realm of instruction. Some curriculum specialists have also gotten into the act through their effort to develop segmental management systems, such as curriculum mapping and curriculum alignment (English, 1980; Glatthorn, 1987). Curriculum mapping emerged out of a technocratic mentality that views the curriculum as a management tool to be used in "scheduling and configuring resources" and in monitoring and guiding teacher performance as it conforms to pre-identified purposes and objectives (English, 1983). The central purpose of curriculum mapping is tied to the act of identifying and aligning specific mastery objectives. As English (1983) stated, "mapping is a technique for recording time on task data and then analyzing these data to determine the fit to the officially adopted curriculum and assessment testing program" (p. 13). Since the rhetoric of curriculum alignment describes curriculum development as a process requiring a carefully tailored coordination of objectives, learning experiences, and testing procedures, it has a surface appeal. Inevitably, however, curriculum alignment turns out to be little more than a rationalization for teaching to the test, because it tends to bring everything into alignment with the all-encompassing priority of raising test scores. In this way, it brings the act of teaching down to its least common denominator, reducing teaching and learning to instrumental levels and stripping the life experience out of the school curriculum.

THE PROBLEM OF CONTROL IN CURRICULUM HISTORY

During the early decades of the twentieth century, it was not difficult to find definite instances of social control and social efficiency in the operation and justification of the school curriculum. Education writers such as Franklin Bobbitt, W. W. Charters, and David Snedden, as well as collective efforts like the Committee on Economy of Time, all sought to impose an outcome-driven curriculum that dramatically delimited and fragmented the school experience. As discussed earlier, Bobbitt was wedded to an industrial model of schooling that highlighted the standardization of learning products. Decisions regarding what should be included in the curriculum were justified through the method of job analysis, which, as the name implies, itemized specific activities that were part of various "given" areas of adult living. The activities became the objectives in the curriculum; the educator simply had to find the instructional tactic that would best fulfill the objectives. A few other thinkers who were committed to the idea of atomizing the curriculum into specific teachable components were more cautious about drawing the activities of the curriculum directly from what already existed in adult life. Charters (1924), for instance, thought that the nature of the objective should be framed through the wider sights of philosophers and that the technique of job or activity analysis could then be used to carry out these objectives. Bobbitt (1918, 1924), however, advanced no mediating elements and had no qualms about the social predestining qualities of his curriculum. Job analysis was an efficient method that sorted and slotted aspects of society and trained students accordingly, in ways that would insure social harmony and economic prosperity. As noted, this mechanistic model would have its legacy in the later rise of outcome-driven or performance-driven instruction.

While Bobbitt and Charters identified skills and activities that called for efficient and mechanical learning experiences, Snedden (1914) went one step further and spoke directly to the need for the schools to project the probable social and occupational destinies of youth and to prescribe a curriculum that facilitated this destiny for each individual student (Drost, 1977). For Snedden, the curriculum was to be used to prepare students for a specific place and task in society.

In time, however, Snedden was criticized harshly by Dewey (1914; 1915) for attempting to use the school as an instrument of social predestination. Dewey supported a comprehensive vision of schooling that went beyond the utilitarian focus of vocational training, although he very clearly saw the educative powers of vocational learning in the context of social and communal living. Dewey's own lab school, it should be recalled, used social occupations as its unifying curricular theme and in *Schools of Tomorrow* (Dewey & Dewey, 1915), co-written with his daughter Evelyn, he focused on schools that merged technical and vocational studies with a wider social and democratizing vision. In a famous quote, Dewey (1915) declared:

> The kind of vocational education in which I am interested is not one which will "adapt" workers to the existing industrial regime; I am not sufficiently in love with the regime for that. It seems to me that the business of all who would not be educational time-servers is to resist every move in this direction, and to strive for a kind of vocational education which will first alter the existing industrial system, and ultimately transform it. (p. 42)

Dewey made his views clear, though even he, as we shall discuss later, would later be interpreted by various radical commentators as supporting the corporate status quo.

Snedden's views about school were said to have been learned in the classroom of Edward Ross, a sociologist who wrote extensively on the topic of social control in a democracy (Kliebard, 1986; Krug, 1964). Ross hit upon the idea of social control as an antidote to the prevailing Social Darwinism of his time. For Ross, the school, among other institutions, had an obligation to intervene in the society and to stabilize it in the interests of the common welfare. This meant that the school would need to soften its regard for individual aims, reexplore its social role, and ultimately engage in an agenda of social control and social order (as opposed to the laissez-faire images of natural control and natural order).

Predictably, several curriculum scholars have gone on to indict the work of Ross for its strong call to place the individual in the control of the state (Franklin, 1986; Kliebard, 1986; Krug, 1964). Krug (1964), for instance, claimed that Ross saw the school as a mechanism for the calculated management and control of society.

Krug states that Ross described the school as "an economical system of police" (p. 252), a phrase that has since been repeated in subsequent mentions of Ross's work (Bennett & LeCompte, 1990; Franklin, 1986; Giroux, 1983b; Spring, 1988). Like Krug, Kliebard (1986) maintained that Ross conceptualized the good society as one that subjects individuals to state prerogatives and moral mandates of conduct. Similarly, Franklin (1986) characterized Ross as seeking to dominate individuals with a social plan that would impose a strict order of predefined social expectation to which all members of society would be molded.

The indictment against Ross, however, has been challenged. Some of the controversy is, in fact, indicative of the essential problem facing the analysis of control in the school curriculum. Was Ross articulating social control as a mechanism of preserving the status quo, or was he, in the tradition of the experimentalists, advancing lines of control in the service of social insight and self-directed initiative? The difference in intention is significant because it underscores two fundamentally different conceptual grounds. Tanner and Tanner (1990) have argued that Ross perceived the possibility of two fundamentally different types of social control: the traditionalist view of imposition and the progressive view of civic virtue and the release of a collective democratizing movement. According to the Tanners, Ross not only sided with the latter but vigorously attacked the former. They maintain that when Ross stated that schooling was "an economical system of police," he was actually referring to the traditional form of control that was no longer viable in a more modern society. Ross, the Tanners continue, actually sided more closely with Lester Ward's idea that social control should be expressed through enlightened interventionist policies (e.g., universal public education) in the society. In fact, Ross dedicated his first major work, *Social Control* (1901), to Ward, who pronounced the book "at once brilliant and profound" (Ross, 1901, p. xxxv). It should be noted that Ward has been widely acknowledged as a social meliorist (Kliebard, 1986).

The Tanners seem to have a point. Ross was by no means a voice for the status quo. As one of the early fathers of American sociology, he spoke out against social hierarchy in the society and the growing power of the capitalist class. He believed that a kind of social control already existed, exercised through the instruments of class domination in the exploitation of the public trust. Using a criticism worthy of a Marxist, Ross described the imposition of class-bound values as leading to beliefs, customs, and traditions that regulate social conditions and ultimately resist change. Such a social arrangement, according to Ross (1901), was characterized by "the exercise of power by a parasitic class [acting] in its own interest" (p. 376). Thus Ross was moved to draw a firm distinction between "social control," which would facilitate individual liberty and egalitarian mobility, and "class control," which served the interests of the economic elites and led to sharp cleavages among social and economic groups. Social control, which in the social-efficiency tradition reflected the functionalist regard for the static and the conservative, was in Ross's thinking an instrument of change that would celebrate collectivist causes and create new forms of consensus and consciousness.

Interestingly, Franklin (1986) admitted that Ross spoke of "indirect control that operated internally as a natural growth of social interaction" (p. 21) and that Ross favored these forms of control in modern society, but he also claimed that Ross failed to explain how the idea of control by psychological regulation would work. Moreover, Franklin (1986) exposed the racism in Ross's fear of diluting the genetic strain of the American population. It was, in fact, apparently over this very point that Ross lost his appointment at Stanford University: He spoke out publicly about the perils posed to the American standard of living by the Oriental immigration. Ross, it should be noted, denied having made the offending statements (Weinberg, 1972).

Different elements in Ross's work are admittedly difficult to reconcile. Even Kliebard (1986) acknowledged that Ross was "beset by a kind of intellectual schizophrenia" (p. 91), though Kliebard chose to emphasize the less progressive elements of Ross. On the one hand, Ross's scholarship was strained by his failure to explain how agents of control were internalized in the individual and by his purported idealization of an ethnically homogeneous society; on the other, Ross seems to have had a progressive side that undermined the conservative faith in competition (and its accompanying laissez-faire philosophy) and that recognized the role of the state as a potential instrument of social amelioration. Ross sought to counter the repressive hand of class exploitation with the ameliorative hand of the state. He attached no instrumentalism to his idea (an actual method of conduct) and advanced no behavioristic manipulations designed to promote individual and group order. One could argue that he aimed to shape a new form of social control through the formation of public agencies that would replace the coercive controls of the past with a collectivist civic and moral purpose.

These distinctions between various notions of control were also treated by Dewey, who believed that circumscribing boundaries had to be set on a school curriculum for it to fulfill its expressed mission. Dewey openly expressed the idea that the school was a deliberately conceived educative environment that, by virtue of its implied boundaries, carried out a guiding or controlling function. It was clear to Dewey that the impulses of the immature had to be consciously directed through the institutions of society, including, most significantly, the school. But this sense of control was stated positively; it led not to methods of coercion, imposition, and subordination but to a directive framework intended to facilitate the control of individual and collective fate. Such a framework suggested modes of thought and conduct that were based on a vision of society but that ultimately had to be worked out in experience. In this way curriculum theory, although influenced by the society, the nature of the learner, and the subject matter, was, in the final analysis, shaped in the experience—in the actual effort to reconstruct experience for individual and collective enlightenment. The basis of control, then, was in the character of the experience; and the curriculum, as the guiding construct for this experience, offended no principle of freedom if its boundaries were responsive to the values and aims of the society. As Dewey (1916) declared, "the conception of education as a social process and function has no definite meaning until we define the kind of society we have in mind" (p. 97). Thus, while the nature of learning (knowing, reflecting, inquiring) is always fluid and cannot be understood ahead of time, it is nonetheless framed within a directive purpose. For Dewey, curriculum theory was indeed an emergent activity that is continuously reconstructed according to the particulars of the educational situation and a standing philosophical ideal. Growth, in this sense, is only possible if limits are placed on the curriculum, a theme that critical theorists perceive as authoritarian and repressive.

The structure of Dewey's laboratory school exemplified how a social and living education necessitated constraints. As Gutmann (1987) noted, in Dewey's school the idea of creating an embryonic democratic society was tempered by the understanding that such a form could not be totally democratic; the school, for instance, did not treat students and teachers as political and intellectual equals. The concern to design an educative environment led to giving the teacher great authority in curriculum decisions. Youth were perceived as undeveloped and immature, in the process of learning how to translate their inchoate interests into intellectual and emotional control. The school derived its educative potency from providing a "purified medium of action" that was responsive to a continuum of experience. In Dewey's laboratory school, fundamental social occupations were central to intellectual and emotional growth, which involved not only practical skills and mature behavior but also knowledge of subject matter. The development of these competencies was perceived to be anchored in the context of continuously reconstructed experience. The school was artificially designed to eliminate unwanted influences, but the student responses to the environment were to be imbued with the spirit of membership in a community and with the sense that school was a place to conduct a life.

Yet several revisionist historians and radical curriculum theorists have portrayed Dewey as a thinker whose idealistic treatment of democracy led him to advocate an education of conformity to the well-being of the group (Katz, 1971). This sense of conformity is said to have been amenable to industrial priorities and the maintenance of an economic system that required a surplus of unskilled laborers content with their identification with industry (Karier, 1976; Katz, 1971). Some curriculum theorists, such as Grumet (1981), have taken a similar position, advancing the notion that Dewey's philosophy and curriculum theory encouraged adjustment rather than resistance; that his faith in the reconstruction of the school and the society through problem-focused inquiry was, despite the colorful rhetoric, instrumental in nature and conducive to apolitical and conserving activities. Similarly, Giroux and Aronowitz (1985), while not advancing the notion that Dewey supported a curriculum of adjustment, castigated him for being unrealistically optimistic about using the school as an agency for the amelioration of society and for failing to fully understand the class and culture struggles that mark the school experience.

Feinberg (1975) added to the criticism by observing that Dewey and other noteworthy progressives (such as Counts and Rugg) were interested in using the school as a management mechanism for the control of the general population toward some common ends or goals, and that an important function of the school was to place a nationalizing or amalgamating stamp of commonality on each individual. Thus Feinberg (1975) maintained that Dewey's views represented an effort to stabilize and reinforce the status quo. The school, for Dewey, was said to exist for transmissive not transformative purposes—a position that runs counter to the previously mentioned views of Bowers (1987), who faulted Dewey for failing to include any conserving effect in the curriculum.

These charges are difficult to understand because Dewey often characterized the school as an engine for social insight and social improvement. As a progressive-experimentalist, he believed that the guiding principle on schooling was to effect change through the employment of an intelligent and reflective method. He wrote passionately about the tyranny of absolutism and was unequivocally opposed to using the school to maintain special interests, especially those rooted in business and industry or in a narrow sense of nationalism:

> A democratic criterion requires us to develop capacity to the point of competency to choose and make its own career. This principle is violated when the attempt is made to fit individuals in advance for definite industrial callings, selected not on the basis of trained original capacities, but on that of the wealth or social status of parents. . . . Wherever social control means subordination of individuals' activities to class authority, there is a danger that industrial education will be dominated by acceptance of the status quo. (Dewey, 1916, pp. 119–120)

The confusion regarding Dewey's stance on the issue of maintaining the status quo probably has much to do with his belief in using the school to cultivate a unifying and democratic social spirit in the school population. For Dewey, it was clearly important to establish a sense of social cohesion grounded in common issues and tolerance for diversity. Katz (1971) and others have characterized this as oppressive, as a call for conformist behavior. Dewey, however, did not advocate the erosion of diversity as the price of social democracy. For instance, he wrote:

> The Theory of the Melting Pot always gave me rather a pang. To maintain that all the constituent elements, geographical, racial and cultural in the United States, should be put in the same pot and turned into a uniform and unchanging product is distasteful. (Dewey, 1917a, p. 289)

Dewey, contrary to claims, was not blind to the problem of class interest in his analysis of education. In fact, he viewed the school as providing an opportunity for the circulation of social, ethnic, racial, and religious diversity in ways that would help dissolve class lines in the society:

> In order to have a large number of values in common, all the members of the group must have an equable opportunity to receive and to take from others. There must be a large number of shared undertakings

and experiences. Otherwise, the influences which educate some into masters, educate others into slaves. And the experience of each party loses in meaning, when the free interchange of varying modes of life-experience is arrested. A separation into a privileged and a subject-class prevents social endosmosis. (Dewey, 1916, p. 84)

Of course, Dewey did not care much for ideology because he felt that it led to "isms" or allegiances that mitigated against open discourse; nor did he care for argumentation from the perspective of class interest, again because he felt that it was exclusive and de-limiting in nature. He did, however, take seriously the issue of class reproduction through the school:

> It is not enough to see to it that education is not actively used as an instrument to make easier the exploitation of one class by another. School facilities must be secured of such amplitude and efficiency as will in fact and not simply in name discount the effects of economic inequalities. Accomplishment of this end demands not only adequate administrative provision of school facilities but also such modification of traditional ideals of culture, traditional subjects of study and traditional methods of teaching and discipline as will retain all the youth under educational influences until they are equipped to be masters of their own economic and social careers. The ideal is short of execution but the democratic ideal is farcical except as it dominates the public system of education. (Dewey, 1916, p. 98)

Charges of advocating social control and social efficiency, while understandable when leveled against the work of Bobbitt and Snedden, are not so easily defended when applied to the work of Dewey and other progressives. The same could also be said of the similar indictment made against the *Cardinal Principles* report (Commission for the Reorganization of Secondary Education, 1918).

The *Cardinal Principles* report has often been cited as a turning point in American education, primarily because it offered a progressive alternative to the strictly academic curriculum of traditional education. In the report, the idea of instruction through the tactic of mental discipline was replaced with a search for life activities responsive to individual and social needs. Many progressives hailed the report for attempting to democratize schools by emphasizing the comprehensive education of all youth in a setting that provided for both specialized and common learning. Cremin (1955) saw the *Cardinal Principles* report as a unique American effort to educate all youth in a unified setting in ways that allowed for both sociocivic education (general education) and specialized academic instruction. Such a system contrasted markedly with the separatist, dual system that existed in Europe.

Several historians, however, have characterized the *Cardinal Principles* report in quite a different light. Krug (1964), for instance, claimed that the report was more directly attuned to the function of social efficiency than to the mission of democracy. The differentiated programs that the report supported within a unified setting are described as tracking systems that fulfilled the social-efficiency objective of social predestination and social control. He also claimed that the content of the report was dominated by Kingsley, who, as a protegé of Snedden, sought to impose social-engineering objectives in order to use the school to fit individuals into society. Yet the *Cardinal Principles* document garnered little approval from prominent thinkers who worked expressly in the tradition of social efficiency. Snedden, for instance, had a low opinion of the report because he favored the separation of academic and vocation education—the very idea that the *Cardinal Principles* report repudiated. Bobbitt, as reported by Krug (1972) himself, was unhappy with the vagueness of the report, so much so that he developed an instructional program that itemized the original seven objectives of the report into more specific and detailed abilities. Inexplicably, Krug portrayed this action as evidence of Bobbitt's support for the *Cardinal Principles,* even though the very idea of applying the mechanism of job analysis to the report was very clearly an abuse of the report's central focus. Advocacy for the procedure of job analysis is found nowhere in the report, despite the considerable support it enjoyed at the time.

Spring (1972) has followed in the tradition of Krug by arguing that the *Cardinal Principles* statement upheld a social-efficiency model of schooling that allowed for the exercise of corporate prerogatives in the life of the school. Spring criticized the specialized function of the curriculum supported in the report as leading to a culture of differentiation that is inequitable and unjust. Spring, however, also attacked the common learnings feature of the curriculum supported in the report. To Spring, these unifying functions—which he characterized as extracurriculum events, school assemblies, and athletic endeavors—were simply means for creating a corporate feeling in the school. Such an effort to bring about a corporate feeling in the school, he believed, simply reflected social control and the socialization of individuals to conform to the existing

society. Again we encounter the double-bind argument: The specialized function of the curriculum is repressive because it differenti-
ates between social groups; but the common curriculum is also repressive because, in essence, it does *not* differentiate between
social groups.

Among the common learning elements supported in the
Cardinal Principles report was a general education curriculum that
offered students participation in a common discourse dealing with
issues related to their world and to the task of citizenship. Such a
curriculum was manifestly designed to broaden understanding of
sociocivic concerns and to help youth make intelligent decisions
about themselves, their communities, and their society. The purpose was to give young people control of their own destinies, not to
place them under the control of some regulatory authority tied into
the preservation of a socioeconomic determinism. The term *efficiency* was used in the report, but it took on a meaning that was
contrary to the biases in the efficiency-driven ideas of Bobbitt and
Charters. As Wraga (1991) explained, the term was used in a manner that transcended the standard denotation of economy and cost-
saving. It was widened to mean broad competence and was often
couched in the context of a sociocivic intelligence. In fact, as Tanner
and Tanner (1990) reported, even Dewey, who spoke so powerfully
against scientism and the scientific management initiatives that enjoyed popularity during the early decades of this century, maintained that the idea of social efficiency was useful when it described
the wide release of human insight and collective wisdom in the conduct of the population:

> In the broadest sense, social efficiency is nothing less than that social-
> ization of mind which is actively concerned in making experiences
> more communicable; in breaking down the barriers of social stratifi-
> cation which make individuals impervious to the interests of others.
> (Dewey, 1916, pp. 120–121)

For Dewey, social efficiency, like the broader notion of social control, connoted the spirit and meaning of social intelligence and
the understanding that every social arrangement requires an intelligent subordination of nature to social rule. Thus, as Dewey (1916)
continued:

> Social efficiency means neither more nor less than capacity to share
> in a give and take of experience. It covers all that makes one's own

experience more worth while to others, and all that enables one to participate more richly in the worthwhile experiences of others. (p. 120)

The activity-based recommendations for the curriculum that were supported in the *Cardinal Principles* report were in alignment with Dewey's idea of efficiency (Wraga, 1991), even though the activity-oriented mode of content recommended in the report also suited behavioristic social-efficiency priorities and, in the end, foreshadowed the problems that the life adjustment movement would encounter in the 1940s and 1950s.

Misperception of the meaning of control has also tainted the interpretation of such important curriculum figures as Newlon and Caswell. As mentioned earlier, Newlon won considerable praise in the literature for his work in schoolwide curriculum revision and his effort to make teachers part of curriculum reform. Still, Pinar and Grumet (1981) labeled Newlon a managerial expert who sought to impose his own socially efficient procedures on the school. (This issue was treated in Chapter 1.) Regarding the idea of control, Newlon (1939b) was forthright in proclaiming that "popular education is an effective instrument of social control" (p. 4). Repeatedly, however, Newlon framed this notion of control in the language of democracy; he expressed the desire to wrest control from the special interests and give it to the people. For Newlon, the aim of education was to equip youth and communities of youth with the skills of thoughtful self-direction (a kind of control) in a process of "experience reconstructing experience." Newlon also understood the limitations of the political process and the democratic sense of interdependence, which suggest certain limits and forms of authority.

Interestingly, Hollis Caswell's ideas about social control have been treated more fairly by radical critics. As Franklin (1986) indicated, Caswell saw the school as a place where social cooperation and understanding could be developed in an instructional context— a stance more sensitive to student concerns and social causes than the social-efficiency doctrine of Bobbitt and Charters. Caswell also cautioned against the intrusion of business interests into the conduct of the school and sought to instill in students the democratizing skills of inquiry, cooperation, self-integrity, open-mindedness, and other "generalized controls of conduct." In an effort to help develop a curriculum organized around the problems and concerns of youth in contemporary society, Caswell made use of and helped to popularize the concepts of scope and sequence. These two concepts were used to integrate the content of the curriculum across and within grade levels. This is precisely the kind of gridding of the curriculum that has moved radical critics to claim that curriculum development destroys the opportunity for diverse and phenomenological forms of experience. However, the key structural component in Caswell's view of curriculum planning was the concept of experience. In Seguel's (1966) words, to Caswell "the elements of the curriculum process are experiential, and a major characteristic of human experience is human purpose and human control" (p. 164). To the extent that the learner's conduct is self-determined and consciously reflected on, the learner gains control over his or her life; Caswell sought to cultivate this, but within the framework of a democratizing ideal that was cooperative and tolerant in spirit. Even Krug (1950), who was among the first scholars to identify the problem of social control and social efficiency, wrote a book on curriculum planning that was very much in the tradition of Caswell. In this work, Krug emphasized the role of developmental tasks, school objectives, and scope and sequence considerations in the curriculum. Interestingly, Krug has not been criticized on this "traditionalist" point of social control. Yet the tenor of Krug's views on curriculum planning is not substantively different from Caswell's. Krug (1950) observed: "The curriculum problem may be stated as follows: How can we, the people, direct educational change in an orderly manner along lines of desired objectives?" (p. 23).

Finally, the meaning of control in Tyler's work has also been misrepresented. As discussed in Chapter 2, the popularity of Tyler's rationale has been explained in part as resulting from a traditional urge to use the curriculum as a management device. According to Pinar (1978), the four questions in the rationale signal a "managerial concern with smooth operations" (p. 23). However, the charge of "smooth operations," which implies a kind of reductionist and efficiency function, is peculiar because the rationale is a guiding framework for curriculum *change*. It should be recalled that Tyler used the rationale in developing the framework of the Eight-Year Study, in which he and his associates advised and helped to assess the curriculum development work conducted in experimental high schools, all of which were united in their desire to reject traditional programs (Tanner & Tanner, 1979). These were hardly schools concerned with smooth operations. It should also be noted that, by its design, the rationale raises continuous questions about school operations and insists that these questions be responsive to emerging issues regarding the learner, the society, and the subject matter within a psychophilosophic context. Again, these are hardly a pre-condition for smooth operations in the sense conveyed by Pinar. It is also clear that the rationale, as it was used in the Eight-Year Study, was not based on the presupposition that administrative authority is the exclusive ground for curriculum decision making. Rather, according to Tyler (1984), he and his colleagues:

> decided that the curriculum could not be decided at the district level or in the principal's office and then be given to teachers to implement. Hence, in the second year, the thirty schools established committees for the teachers to plan and develop curriculum. (p. 98)

Nevertheless, the effort to shackle the Tyler rationale to a managerial function continues. Pinar and Grumet (1981), for instance, declared that the rationale has sought to placate involvement groups in the school, although no evidence is provided to show such an effect. Indeed, Tyler (1981) has valued discourse among the main determiners of the curriculum (principals, teachers, students) and has argued rather vigorously for the place of teacher artistry and personal style in the development of learning experiences. Contrary to the claims of Pinar and Grumet, the rationale identified the problems to which curriculum developers should be responsive; gave rise to leading questions and to the investigation of historically supported sources of data; and, by highlighting the importance of studies of the learner, the society, and subject matter, aimed to integrate the diverse interest groups concerned with curriculum.

The Tyler rationale is in the tradition of Dewey because it frames curriculum planning as an inquiry process that considers ends as open points for deliberation while simultaneously advocating sensitivity to the nature of the learner, the values and aims of the society, and the reflective reformulation of the subject matter. One may criticize Tyler for failing to discuss philosophical considerations in a more comprehensive framework (as several commentators have done), but it is wrong to argue that the Tyler rationale seeks to control educational ends in ways that extinguish the variety of lived experiences. The rationale encourages the main determiners of the curriculum to take charge of the curriculum; it supplies guiding questions and sources not to suffocate artful initiative, but to lend a fundamental vision of growth and movement toward an ideal. It is not and should not be the only model for curriculum development, as Tyler himself declared. However, the rationale is neither a mechanism of social efficiency nor an administrative procedure anchored in technocratic rationality. Its orientation and pattern are quite different from Franklin Bobbitt's curriculum techniques and from modern systems theory. Yet it stands as something more than Tyler's own version for curriculum development because it represents the curriculum field's historical commitment to curriculum development as a problem-solving process (Tanner, 1982).

SUMMARY

Radical commentators who deal with the issue of control in the curriculum continue to portray it in only its most behavioristic light. Shaker (1991), for example, states:

> Control depends on . . . the belief that we can fragment experience into discrete components, like objectives, without changing its meaning or oversimplifying its scope. . . . Control suggests, too, that a predictable, student-product emerges from the process of schooling. (p. 168)

Behavioristic ideas of control have led to low-level engagements in the curriculum, ranging from Bobbitt's early advocacy of job analysis to contemporary concerns with time-on-task, effective-teaching strategies, curriculum mapping, and a host of competency-based procedures. But progressive ideas of control, as I have shown in this chapter, encompass qualities that are fundamental to our freedoms. Intelligent self-control and enlightened collective empowerment support the virtues of our democracy. They are forms of conduct that are controlling, but not authoritarian. They are created out of principle, not prescription; out of judgment, not technique; out of the notion of putting people in control, not under control. Progressive scholars in the history of curriculum, such as Ross, Dewey, Newlon, Caswell, and Tyler, recognized that freedom and democracy are very much obligated to intelligent control.

CHAPTER 4

THE CASE OF THE PROGRESSIVE-EXPERIMENTALIST

No man or mind was ever emancipated merely by being left alone. Removal of formal limitations is but a negative condition; positive freedom is not a state but an act which involves methods and instrumentalities for control of conditions.

John Dewey

The progressive-experimentalist tradition has been fundamental to the general development of curriculum thought. Given such an influence, the curriculum field can be described as an early effort to carve out an expressive educational theory for the American public schools, one that placed an increased emphasis on social aims. It was also a movement, however, that sustained a powerful criticism against traditional forms of instruction and, contrary to popular belief, engaged in a penetrating social analysis of inequity and injustice in the American public schools.

Many radical critics have ignored the critical nature of the thinking among progressives and have mischaracterized the experimentalist tradition as one that is beholden to a technocratic rationality. Such a regard for overt rationalism has allegedly resulted in the ascent of an instrumentalist research methodology and instructional slant in curriculum studies.

As will be explained, experimentalist thought not only put forth a sweeping and strongly worded social criticism but also argued for an educational theory to justify the construction of certain learning environments. This conception of the school as a deliberately constructed educative environment included mediating variables that lent direction, not prescription, to the school experience. Much of so-called dominant curriculum thought, to which the radical interpretation has attached social efficiency and managerial priorities, operated on the experimentalist plane. Its leadership arose from a historical curriculum scholarship that Pinar and others have mis-labeled as traditional. Yet, ironically, many of its generalities, especially as they were developed by Dewey, are beginning to find a home even among radical ranks. Part of this awakening is attributable to the failure of radical theory to fashion a discourse that speaks to programmatic concerns regarding the development of certain skills, knowledge, and values in the school. The limits of protest as theory inevitably led to a demand for more practical deliberations about curriculum; increasingly, the pragmatic focus of Dewey has come into style, although in a manner that is less than precise in its treatment of Dewey.

THE EXPERIMENTALIST FRAMEWORK: THE LEARNER, THE SOCIETY, AND THE SUBJECT MATTER

Early in the twentieth century, educational thought was mired in a conflict between subject-centered and child-centered approaches to curriculum making. Dewey (1902a) described this condition in *The Child and the Curriculum:*

> The easy thing is to seize upon something in the nature of the child, or upon something in the developed consciousness of the adult, and insist upon that as the key to the whole problem. When this happens a really serious practical problem—that of interaction—is transformed into an unreal, and hence insoluble theoretical problem. Instead of seeing the educative steady and as a whole, we see conflicting terms. We get the case of the child v. the curriculum; of the individual nature v. social culture. Below all other divisions in pedagogic opinion lies this opposition. (pp. 4–5)

Distressed by the either/or mentality of thinking among education scholars, Dewey attempted to create a new line of argumentation by supporting the consideration of three fundamental factors that interdependently make up what he called the educative process. These factors included (1) the nature of the learner, (2) the values and aims of society, and (3) reflectively organized subject matter. Dewey believed that if all curriculum initiatives reflected these factors, as they existed organically, significant steps might be taken toward achieving a common ground for problem solving in education.

Dewey, like all progressive-experimentalists, was influenced by the pragmatic movement in American philosophy. Pragmatism, which supported the role of empiricism in philosophy, was a clear rejection of absolutism and a clear promotion of scientific methodology as the primary method of human intelligence. By emphasizing the value of reflective thinking and by seeing transformative effects (for the individual and the society) in the ongoing reconstruction of experience and knowledge, Dewey advanced a brand of empiricism that used the scientific method as an instrument for social and moral renewal. He tempered the scientific method by reformulating it in the context of democratic idealism. As a result, Dewey often spoke of the powers of reflective thought as they related to the improvement of democratic social conditions. Given these assumptions, the task of the school was to develop persons with an experimental habit of mind and with the ethical disposition to advance the cooperative and social aims of democracy. Thus learning in school was a process of social growth, always in the process of becoming, never achieving a state of completeness, and measuring success in terms of its movement toward democratic idealism. Such an emphasis is the opposite of critical theory's emphasis on the nonrational or even antirational factors in human behavior.

Beyond the influence of the experimentalists, much of the early progressive pulse in education can be described as a recognition of the need for schooling to take greater stock in the learner and to bring subject matter and learning strategies in line with the demands of the learner's life. During the early decades of this century, there was a romantic child-centered element within the progressive movement that advocated activity-centered learning for its own sake. There was also, however, an effort to balance this extreme with innovative studies that were more scientifically controlled.

Seeing the development of knowledge in the curriculum field as an incremental process, Tanner and Tanner (1980) have contended that the three fundamental factors mentioned above (the learner, the society, and the subject matter) have evolved into the conceptual underpinning for a problem-solving paradigm for the field. Besides encompassing the three fundamental factors, such a paradigm also posits four essential functions in the process of curriculum development: (1) it identifies educational objectives; (2) it selects the means for attaining them; (3) it organizes the means into a plan; and (4) it evaluates the outcomes realized. As Tanner and Tanner furthered indicated, these were precisely the elements that went into a long line of curriculum research. One could argue, as others have (Jickling, 1988), that the Tanners did not identify a paradigm in the Kuhnian sense. What seems clear, however, is that an experimentalist line of thought has been identified and that its influence in the curriculum field has been significant.

The conception of the learner, for instance, is one of the fundamental dividing lines between behavioristic and experimentalist orientations in the curriculum. As mentioned, there was an early tendency among progressives to deal with the learner in ways that were child-centered in the extreme. The idea of activity, in and of itself, was seen as the central objective of education; "learning by doing" became the banner under which these early progressives made a virtue of virtually any task that the child was committed to perform in the classroom. The idea was that open, meaningful, and happy school experiences could only be achieved by elevating the status of activity per se in an unstructured and unplanned environment. Several early progressives were attracted to this idea because it meant that the child had finally gained due consideration in the calculations of the curriculum and that active experience in learning would gain a foothold in an institution that had long equated formal education with a stale uniformity of low-level instruction and repressed physical motion. Activity indeed seemed to be a logical key to freeing the student from repressive authority and from the dull instructional uniformity of rote and recitation.

Although progressive-experimentalists were among those who participated in the reaction against the abstract and lifeless quality of early timeworn forms of instruction, they also feared the counter-extreme of child-centeredness and the sentimentalization of learning as a process without boundaries. Dewey (1929a), usually a gentle critic, issued a strongly worded criticism.

> There is a present tendency in so-called advanced schools of educational thought to say, in effect, let us surround pupils with certain materials, tools, appliances, etc. and let pupils respond to these things according to their own desires. Above all let us not suggest any end or plan to students; let us not suggest to them what they shall do, for that is an unwarranted trespass upon their sacred intellectual individuality since the essence of such individuality is to set up ends and aims. Now such a method is really stupid. For it attempts the impossible, which is always stupid; and it misconceives the conditions of independent thinking. (p. 153)

For Dewey, learning necessitated guidance, direction, order, and control, all within the common spirit of the social group; without these controlling tendencies, the school could not systematically foster the conditions for self-renewal and improvement. In other words, unless one turned to the systematic needs of personal and social reconstruction, which presumes a purposive direction, life in school and society would actually become more stagnate and more easily victimized by mechanical, routinized, and authoritarian elements. As Bowers (1984) explained, neo-romantic schools that emphasize spontaneous self-expression can contribute to a relativizing of authority that threatens to collapse into authoritarianism:

> It is not that alternative-free schools promote authoritarianism; it is more a question whether the values of freedom, equality, and individual centeredness, when made the starting point of the educational process, are allowed to overpower curricular and pedagogical practices that develop the intellectual discipline necessary for resisting authoritarianism in its more modern forms. (p. 23)

Among progressive-experimentalists, the idea of the learner had to be balanced with a vision of a society; the school, after all, was an agency committed to the improvement of the society, upholding the civic mission of providing a common universe for social discourse and cultural understanding. Thus, to these progressives, the learner was perceived as a socially conscious and democratically inspired thinker whose intelligence could grasp scientific methodology and use it to solve problems. This stands in contradistinction to the behaviorists, who perceived the learner as an organism to be manipulated and controlled, through stimulus–response reactions, by external devices and procedures. This is also quite different from the conception of the learner supported by so-called postcritical theorists, which, in most cases, is individualistic in its concern for self-expression, self-consciousness, and self-meaning. Indeed, as other curriculum theorists have argued, the postcritical regard for the self-encounter is reminiscent of the child-centered qualities that marked some early progressive curriculum initiatives.

Society is also essential to the experimentalist tradition in curriculum. In a democratic society, the schools must embody the principles and values of democratic living. Bode, Dewey, Childs, and Rugg all promoted the idea that the school is a place to conduct the life of a democracy. They were also forthright in clarifying what constituted democracy in the school, making a case against the intermingling of broad democratic goals with narrow nationalistic ones. During times of presumed national crisis, such intermingling tends to become exacerbated and the pursuit of narrow nationalistic goals supersedes all other concerns. This is exactly the condition that prevailed during the post-*Sputnik* reforms. In 1916, Dewey cautioned that "one of the fundamental problems in education is set by the conflict of a nationalistic and a wider social aim" (p. 97). Dewey expressed a desire to place educational theory in the context of the social priorities of a democracy, as opposed to its industrial, economic, or military priorities. This desire was a consistent theme in the progressive literature. Bode, Newlon, Caswell, Counts, Rugg, and Tyler were all openly critical of the role that nationalistic forces and institutions might play in the school, a position that contradicts the radical contention that such thinkers played into the hands of the corporate status quo.

There is also a matter of emphasis that divides thinkers on the role of democracy in the schools. Radical theorists, for instance, have criticized progressives for failing to offer a substantive economic and social-class analysis of the school's role in solidifying or perpetuating inequalities. Giroux and Aronowitz (1985), for instance, stated that Dewey had a "clear idea of what schools ought to be" but "avoided making a social and political analysis of what schools actually are" (p. 9); Karier (1976) observed that Dewey "consistently stood against a class analysis of American society" (p. 188). Similarly, Feinberg (1975) noted that a few progressives flirted with a class analysis but that the prevailing message from progressives was functionalist in orientation. And, as discussed, other early progressive thinkers, such as Newlon and Tyler, have been cast as social-efficiency experts who not only failed to understand the oppressive dimensions of schooling but also actually worked in the interests of this oppression (Franklin, 1986; Pinar, 1978; Pinar & Grumet, 1981).

To be sure, progressives such as Dewey, while offering ample warning about using the school for repressive purposes, were more interested in using the school for social gain and insight than for economic leveling. "In the school," noted Dewey (1902b), "the typical occupations followed are freed from all economic stress. The aim is not the economic value of the products, but the development of social power and insight" (p. 18). Moreover, many progressives, especially Bode, were cautious about using the school as an instrument to promote specific social reform policies, no matter how noble such policies might appear. In Bode's (1938a) view, such a course would commit educators to employing conditioning strategies to direct the school toward a policy fixed in advance of conclusions reached by democratic procedures. Bode's position reflected the experimentalists' caution about using the school to impose specific ideological patterns on youth. This is essentially the argument that was used by Bode (1935a, 1935b), Dewey (1934), and others against the social reconstructionism of Counts. Clearly, the cautionary attitude toward ideology expressed by Dewey and Bode runs counter to the ideological emphasis so apparent in the critical theory perspective. This might help to explain why Giroux (1988a) has ignored the clear instrumentalism that marked the work of Dewey, Childs, and Bode (and even, to some degree, Counts) in favor of categorizing each as a social reconstructionist.

All this leads to another distinctive feature in the experimentalist-progressive tradition—its support for the unifying function of the school and the factors that lend social cohesiveness to a pluralist society. Dewey and Mann, for instance, supported the common school as an amalgamating agency in the society. They argued that common and shared experiences should be used for selective transmissive purposes, but they also maintained that these same experiences were essential for cultivating the social discourse and sense of community needed for growth and social correction. In other words, the common school could be used for conserving what is worth conserving and for transforming what needs to be changed. Unfortunately, the high regard that progressives had for a comprehensive concept of schooling, which included a common learning or general education component, has been maligned for leading to the highly selective and inequitable system of curriculum tracking. Even the American comprehensive high school, which was a uniquely progressive idea, has been impugned for fostering an organizational and instructional climate amenable to tracking (Nasaw, 1979; Oakes, 1985).

Commentators such as Oakes (1985) have reinterpreted the comprehensive high school as providing a setting for curriculum differentiation that inevitably leads to different learnings for different socioeconomic groups. However, to imply, as Oakes does, that the comprehensive high school is a mechanism for the systematization of social and instructional inequities is to distort the character of its design and purpose. Indeed, one could argue that the conduct of the comprehensive school has been rendered corrupt by an overwhelming desire to stress only academic education and by a call to sort and slot the student population into ability groups. One could also argue that at least part of the corruption of the comprehensive school has been accomplished at the hands of its staunchest advocates, as in the case of James B. Conant (1959), who favored the education of the most academically inclined and openly advanced the need for comprehensive schools to differentiate instruction according to ability levels.

It should also be understood, however, that the theoretical design of the comprehensive high school, as it was fashioned in the *Cardinal Principles* document (Commission for the Reorganization of Secondary Education, 1918; see Chapter 3) and in the writings of various progressive scholars such as Dewey and Counts, is hostile to tracking and other forms of social segregation. The comprehensive school is a multipurpose institution that derives its identity from its stated unifying function. It consists of several interrelated curricular spheres, including the macrocurricular functions of general education, specialized education, exploratory education, and enrichment education. Thus it should be made clear that tracking is an abuse in a comprehensive high school setting; it is not logically or systemically linked to the design function of the comprehensive high school. Its specializing function cannot and should not be confused with an agenda to differentiate the student population into inequitable categories of instruction (Wraga, 1991). The specialized facet of the curriculum was designed to offer learning experiences for preprofessional and professional preparation, including college preparatory studies and studies that might lead to immediate employment opportunities.

The irony is that the rise of tracking is indicative of a general failure to abide by a comprehensive school model. Tracking occurs mostly in stratified academic high schools that have repudiated the multipurpose tradition of the comprehensive model. This phenomenon has been the result of various sociopolitical factors that have kept the high schools from embracing a more comprehensive concept of schooling. The nationalism of the Cold War and post-*Sputnik* period, the economic retrenchment driving the back-to-basics movement, and the technoindustrial anxieties associated with the Reagan era all elicited "reforms" that emphasized discipline-centered education valuing ability-based academic stratification.

As an ideal model, the comprehensive school, with its multiple curriculum focus and its expressed commitment to common learning, is actually an antidote to tracking. In fact, it should also be noted that support for the comprehensive school came from progressives who did not want the American schools to follow the elitist structure of the dual system used in Europe. Counts is a good example of this. He was an enthusiastic advocate of the comprehensive school, even though he understood the perils of tracking that were unfortunately associated with many comprehensive schools. Yet for Counts (1930), the comprehensive high school was an ideal that would help bring together students from all classes, races, and religions and prolong the period of common schooling begun in the public elementary school. Counts, whose concerns about socioeconomic injustices were clear, believed that the comprehensive school would help promote social mobility and develop the dispositions needed for diverse population groups to live in a common democracy.

During the period marked by the Cold War and the Soviet space challenge, Conant (1959) operated out of the same belief and used his considerable authority to support the comprehensive high school in the face of the political and media call to restructure the public schools according to the dual European model. For Conant, there was no need for a radical repatterning of the public school structure, a view that did much to reduce the pressure to imitate the dual system used in Europe and the Soviet Union. Like Counts before him, Conant opted for a comprehensive concept of schooling that aimed to fulfill the academic, social, vocational, and personal needs of all youth in one setting.

Yet even in the light of this effort to keep the schools from embracing an openly fragmented and socially stratified system, critics such as Feinberg (1989) have dismissed Conant as the architect of the "military–industrial education establishment," the person who proposed a dual system of academic education for suburban youth and vocational education for urban youth. Again, had Conant opted for the dual system advanced by Arthur Bestor and Hyman Rickover, his fate would have been sealed as the representative voice of the military–industrial complex. He, of course, did quite the opposite; yet he suffers from the same treatment. As mentioned, since Conant's idea for the comprehensive high school was built around a subject curriculum and around a plea to serve the so-called academically inclined through ability groups, he partially deserves the "Cold War warrior" label sometimes given to him. This accusation, however, must be tempered with a realization of what might have been without Conant's intervention.

To progressives-experimentalists, the values and aims of society act as both sources of and influences on the curriculum. When they are contemplated in relation to the other factors, especially the nature of the learner, they provide vital guidance for curriculum reform. This is a practical and constructive vision—very much a far cry from the negativity that is so basic to critical theory.

The organization of subject matter in the curriculum is another central concern of the progressive tradition. Here the Spencerian question that asks what knowledge is most worthwhile is of continuing relevance. To progressives the subject matter should not, in fact cannot, be prearranged into specialized and separate provinces of knowledge. It must be formulated in concert with emergent experience, attuned to the struggles and satisfactions of personal and social development. Many of the teaching models that grew out of behavioristic influences ignored the subject matter as an analytical element, emphasizing instead procedural methods that could effectively be used with any subject matter; critical theorists, on the other hand, place a strong emphasis on the subject matter, believing that certain knowledge bases are disseminated for political purposes. Yet they generally fail to identify a framework for making subject-matter decisions in the curriculum.

In American education, the curriculum, especially in the secondary school, has typically turned on the mastery of an isolated and fragmented discipline-centered knowledge base. Progressive-experimentalists acknowledge the role of the specialist in influencing what is taught through the curriculum. This influence, however, must be set within the context of the immature learner and larger societal issues, not promoted as the ruling and exclusive element in curriculum development. As Tyler (1949) explained it, the subject specialist must relate the subject matter to the curriculum in ways that contribute to the education of the young citizen or nonspecialist. This is in alignment with Dewey's position that the subject matter should be incorporated into the attitudes and the actions of the pupils as they seek to better understand and better control the social conditions under which they live. The subject matter has no value in and of itself; it exists in concert with the nature of the learner and the value base of the society.

In combining the three factors that Dewey isolated, we are provided with a kind of test against which school proposals can be analytically judged. Presseisen (1985), in fact, has used these very factors to evaluate the content of the major national education reports published during the early 1980s. I engaged in a similar analysis in my review of the curriculum reforms espoused in the most influential education reforms documents of the past half-century (Hlebowitsh, 1990). Even the basic dimensions of the various reform epochs that have marked American education since midcentury can be appraised in these terms. The post-*Sputnik* initiatives, for example, violated each of the three factors by constructing a view of the learner that was built in the image of a scholar-specialist, by emphasizing nationalistic rather than democratic concerns in the school, and by formulating subject matter that was discipline-centered to the extreme—fashioned along highly abstract and technical lines. The humanizing initiatives of the late 1960s and early 1970s, which included the popular open-education concept, also violated these factors. Generally speaking, the nature of the learner was romanticized during this period (which allowed much that we know about learners to go ignored), the goals of the society were phrased in only the most decorous and vague humanistic terms, and the subject matter was left to its own devices—typically leading the school to embrace activity as subject matter. The proliferation of electives and student-centered courses, which followed no clear theme, and the embrace of various activity-centered approaches defined the nature of curriculum development at the time. The back-to-basics movement of the mid-1970s ignored the nature of the learner through its reductionist skill-development agenda; presented no vision of society; and incorporated no real subject matter, as skill-drill took center stage. Among the criticisms of the back-to-basics movement was that it provided children with no body of culture or subject matter, opting instead for the reductionist notion of skill inculcation.

Tanner and Tanner (1980) have argued that the three factors are the products of an evolution of thought in the curriculum field that can be fashioned into a framework for current curriculum deliberations. In attempting to take curriculum development initiatives that are responsive to the learner, for instance, curricularists might ask the school to examine the developmental literature, to survey the interests and social needs of youth, and perhaps even to take into account the more phenomenological aspects of student's life. Similarly, the demand to account for the values of the society in the school curriculum might point toward certain democratic processes in school life, such as social cooperation and community-based learning. Critical thinking, racial and ethnic tolerance, communicative competence, community spiritedness, and a general ability to control one's own destiny and that of the society in an intelligent manner would also be reinforced. In formulating the subject matter of the curriculum, curricularists could look to the learner and to the society in answering the all-important question of what knowledge is most worthwhile. Even where the subject matter is prefashioned, as in some specialized curriculum contexts (e.g., algebra, carpentry), the way this subject matter is dealt with could be related to democratic processes through the use of a teaching methodology that recognizes the importance of the learner and the society. Where various psychophilosophical traditions have conflicting views on the nature of the learner, evidence would have to be brought to bear in justifying each espoused view, and care would have to be taken in seeing that the nature of the learner is viewed in relation to the society and the subject matter. The nature of the learner, in this respect, is always colored with the idealism of democracy.

PRAGMATISM AND THE CURRICULUM

Like experimentalism itself, American pragmatism is a philosophy that uses the scientific method as its chief means of inquiry and understanding, democracy as its value orientation, and evolution as its view of humanity and the world (Childs, 1956). The progenitors of pragmatic thought in American philosophy (typically viewed as Peirce, James, and Dewey) were, of course, not of one mind, and the differences between them, especially between Peirce and James, were considerable. These differences notwithstanding, the curriculum field was able to borrow much from the broad themes of pragmatism, including its denunciation of absolute truth, its faith in self-determined behavior, and its push for the application of a rational and creative intelligence to the improvement of social conditions. Curriculum thought was most profoundly influenced by these broad factors as they were integrated in Dewey's instrumentalism. As the chief axiologist of pragmatism, Dewey offered a social reformer's view of schooling in America.

Despite his bald instrumentalism, Dewey is currently undergoing a kind of reconstruction with many radicals and is increasingly finding a favorable place in their argumentation. Among many prominent radical writers, there is general agreement that Dewey's writings are more closely attuned to the themes of critical theory than not, quite contrary to the treatment afforded to Dewey by radical revisionist historians (see Chapter 3). Giroux and Aronowitz (1985), for instance, claim that "Dewey's educational thought closely approximates the best of Marxist and radical educational theory" (p. 10). Statements on Dewey's importance to radical theory can also be found in McLaren (1989), Apple (1979), Shor (1986), and Giroux (1988b), to name just a few. Among these writers, Dewey is embraced at a high level of generality (as a thinker who was committed to social mutuality, to community discourse for social correction, and to an experiential–reconstructive theory of education). Yet in most cases, this recognition of Dewey is not fully developed in terms of his pragmatism or instrumentalism. If it were, many radicals would have to either reject much of Dewey or substantially modify their positions. Such a problem has, in fact, created wide ripple effects, particularly in the attempt to reconcile Dewey's work with critical theory perspectives as opposed to so-called traditional curriculum perspectives. This is especially difficult because practical curriculum theory, which was an essential component of Dewey's pragmatism, is the very evil against which critical curriculum theorists have reacted, ultimately rejecting it as the inspiration of an instrumental rationality. Such discrepancies are crucial because they reveal a treatment of Dewey (and of the wider curriculum literature) that circumvents Dewey's pragmatism (Hlebowitsh, 1992).

The overarching historical concern of pragmatism is the relation of knowledge and cognition to action and conduct. The central element of analysis among pragmatists is behavior, as it is reflectively reformulated in a context that aims to create a vision of progress and improvement. To return to an earlier theme, pragmatism represents, in Peirce's words, a concern for "conduct controlled by adequate deliberation" (quoted in Morris, 1970, p. 10). In such a scenario, learning how to think and act has to do with "learning how to control experimentally our interactions with the environment" (Childs, 1956, p. 24). Thus it should be clear that pragmatism does not endorse an engineering attitude toward action that could be translated into a fixed and closed system of truth. Although pragmatism relies on rational thinking, it is informed by a democratic value base that acts to "unstiffen," to use James's term, its bases of truth and inquiry. As James (1907) observed, "The difference between pragmatism and rationalism . . . is that for rationalism reality is ready-made and complete for all eternity, while for pragmatism it is still in the making, and awaits part of its complexion from the future" (p. 167). Peirce's original construction of the pragmatic maxim supported this flexibility through the value that it placed on the construction of concepts as experiential operations, through the emphasis it attached to general levels of conduct (kinds of actions and experience, not single actions or experiences), and through the concern it showed for the social and collective effects of behavior, as opposed to individualistic effects (Morris, 1970)—a point on which Peirce differed with James. Interestingly, it is precisely the flexibility of the pragmatic tradition in experimentalist thought that seems to have been ignored in the radical critique. The forces of Peirce's pragmatic maxim are primary, for instance, in the Tyler rationale, where the pragmatic concern for behavioral effects is essential but where general levels of conduct prevail.

For pragmatists, uncertainty is a highly practical matter. Since the uncertainty of life constitutes a large share of the problematic in life, pragmatism looks at present experiences as emerging events of social evolution. In doing so, it takes the promise of social evolution out of the plane of simple trial and error and into the plane of intelligently regulated actions working in accordance with desired democratic values (Childs, 1956). "We always live at the time we live," wrote Dewey (1938b), "and not at some other time, and only by extracting at each present time the full meaning of each present experience are we prepared for doing the same in the future" (p. 51). In this way, our histories, to paraphrase Dewey, are histories of the present and out futures are generated out of the struggles with the present. Out of this struggle come the reconstruction of experience and the reconfiguration of knowledge and conduct as they express themselves in the full force of their consequences in our lives.

The premium placed in pragmatism on the transactional relation between the individual and the environment has led its critics to label it as narrow, utilitarian, and conservative. As a revisionist historian, Greer (1972) stated that Dewey's work could ultimately be "described by his pragmatism which was defined in the context of society's survival" (p. 79) and which was equated, by Greer, with political compromise and socioeconomic stasis (p. 79). Greer's view of pragmatism misunderstands the critical emphasis that it placed on biological change and ignores in Dewey the social commitment to strengthen the creative and intellectual powers of the citizenry in the moral and social life of democracy. Unfortunately, the idea that pragmatism led unimaginatively to a rationalist manipulation of humanity has not been an uncommon criticism. James (1909) noted that:

> Critics treat our view as offering itself exclusively to engineers, doctors, financiers, and men of action generally, who need some sort of a rough and ready Weltanschauung, but have no time or wit to study genuine philosophy . . . a sort of bobtailed scheme of thought, excellently fitted for the man on the street, who naturally hates theory and wants cash returns immediately. (pp. 176–177)

Today pragmatism continues to be characterized as value-free in nature and tethered to a method of inquiry that neutralizes human values as empirical considerations. Because it deals with present conditions, pragmatism is sometimes viewed as lacking the critical scope to reconstruct the present; this inevitably leads to the projection of absolute rationalism as pragmatism. As Apple (1979) stated, "the pragmatic position tends to ignore the possibility that some theories must contradict the present reality and, in fact, must consistently work against it" (p. 133). Apple's concerns seem to be directed to the kind of rule-of-thumb action that emerges from behavioristic empiricism or is directed to an ideological absolutism that insists upon the construction of only one reality. This is not pragmatism; in fact, it is contrary to pragmatism.

Cherryholmes (1988) has given greater nuance to the argument against pragmatism by contrasting what he calls "vulgar pragmatism," which is drawn from an orientation that values functional efficiency, with "critical pragmatism," which he portrays as a poststructuralist strategy to guard against the unreflective reproduction of our traditions. Vulgar pragmatism, which bears no resemblance to the ideals and principles outlined by Dewey, James, and Pierce, is the product of the social-efficiency movement; it is anchored in the pursuit of efficiency in the absence of criticism, actions in the absence of thought, and practice in the absence of theory. Critical pragmatism, however, is also unlike the original construction of pragmatism offered by Dewey, James, and Peirce. While Cherryholmes (1992) acknowledges the varieties of pragmatism elsewhere, his early binary treatment of pragmatism (vulgar v. critical) fails to properly express the pragmatic project as it drove the instrumentalism of Dewey and early progressive mandates for social control and social planning.

In a very strict sense, pragmatism is an ongoing struggle against the present, not a reproduction of it. Apple's call for the contradiction of the present underscores the pragmatists' main point—that our futures grow out of our present problematics and that all education is dependent on the realization of present possibilities for growth. The present is the ground for the reconstruction of experience and insight; and since we do not live in a timeless and static condition, it is necessarily contradicted by emergent disturbances and tensions. The present, as it turns out, also provides an anchor for the past, since, "the present generates the problems which lead us to search the past for suggestion, and which supplies meaning to what we find when we search" (Dewey, 1916, p. 89). Hence the structures and precedents of the past apply only as contributing elements to the present. The consequences of pragmatism, then, help the school to extricate itself from the very universal laws of action and truth that current radical commentators decry, as well as from the ideological emphasis that marks so many radical perspectives. Again, in Dewey's (1917b) words:

> Our life has no background of sanctified categories upon which we may fall back; we rely upon precedent as authority only to our own undoing—for with us there is such a continuously novel situation that final reliance upon precedent entails some class interest guiding us by the nose whither it will. (p. 68)

Several scholars have accentuated the conceptual differences within pragmatism. Prominent among these is Karier (1967), who claimed that the three prominent names associated with pragmatism represent separate strands that form an incomplete, if not fragmented, whole. Peirce, for instance, is described as a logician and realist who sought general principles of conduct, whereas James is described as a humanist who espoused an existential psychologist's view of the world. James's famous radical empiricism, which broadened classical empiricism's boundaries of reality and inquiry, had, according to Karier, a subjective character to it that neither Peirce nor Dewey could accept. Karier's message is that there is little substance to the idea of pragmatism, writ large.

Yet it needs to be stressed that, notwithstanding obvious differences and variations, pragmatism did achieve a kind of synthesis in the curriculum field, much of it represented in the work of Dewey. For instance, although Dewey was not sympathetic to phenomenological approaches, he was excited about the idea of developing an empirical theory free from the burdens of *a priori* rationalism (Dewey, 1929b). He was also impressed with the evolutionary notion of change espoused by pragmatists and the high respect they paid to the cultivation of reflective thinking processes. We witness in Dewey "the coalescence of the critical and the scientific motives of Peirce's pragmatism and the moral implications and ideals of James" (Thayer, 1968, p. 165). This coalescence found expression in the development of the curriculum field, in the vital notion that schools should not only transmit but also reconstruct our social heritage, and in the idea that schooling should cast aside its individualistic focus in favor of more closely relating to the realities of present-day life and community-related social values and aims. In pragmatism we can see the merging of a method and a value orientation that together create the idea of using the school for the renegotiation of culture.

THE SOCIOECONOMIC SITUATION AND EDUCATION

Over the years many radical critics have castigated more mainstream progressive voices in education for ignoring the significance of ideology and economic power in the operation of the schools. Dewey, for instance, whose work often strikes a sympathetic chord with leftist commentators in various other areas of inquiry, is sometimes criticized for not engaging in a full-fledged social-class analysis of American schools (Giroux & Aronowitz, 1985; Karier, 1976). Similarly, Counts and Childs, although acknowledged to be interested in class analysis, are said to have eventually abandoned such concerns as outside the limits of progressive thought (Feinberg, 1975; Greer, 1972). Even Rugg, whose views on schooling were built on a fundamental concern for correcting the social ills of democracy, is characterized as positing a functionalist group theory as an alternative to class analysis (Feinberg, 1975). Also, as indicated, an entire generation of early curriculum scholars in the progressive-liberal tradition has been criticized for its belief in using the school to establish social control and the accompanying condition of socioeconomic stasis (Apple, 1979; Franklin, 1986; Giroux, 1979; Pinar, 1978).

Apparently, in the eyes of radical critics, the leading progressives of the 1930s and 1940s did not quite go far enough in their treatment of social-class concerns. Yet the historical record indicates that such issues were essential to the progressive argument. Contrary to the criticisms lodged against them, most of the prominent progressive thinkers in the field of curriculum did not view the issue of social inequities, as practiced by the school, as unimportant or tangential to curriculum; their writings were as focused on the issue as the writings of radicals today. In fact, many progressive-experimentalists not only criticized class division and economic injustice but also argued for more directed efforts at developing social consciousness and social insight in the school. In this sense, the analysis of the socioeconomic situation was a prerequisite to an argument for curriculum reform in the public schools. Largely as a result of this influence, the public school in the United States sought to universalize schooling through the secondary level and to implement a curriculum that encouraged broadly based social inter-

course—all for the professed objective of creating a more democratic society. To this day, the socioeconomic bias in the U.S. public
schools is the lowest among the schools of industrialized nations, a
fact that is ignored by those who are bent on exploiting the idea of
the school's linkage to social and economic oppression (Husen,
1983; Tanner & Tanner, 1980; Tyler, 1981).

Prior to the rise of progressivism, American schooling was
wedded to a rote and recitation model that elevated the significance
of purely academic learning. Progressive-experimentalists were
among the first to question these priorities and to help shift the
school's instructional orientation away from the intellectual tradition supported by the mental disciplinarians and toward the representation of social concerns and social activities in the curriculum.
In seeking to cultivate the sociocivic function of schooling and the
social service role of the educator, these progressives displayed a
strong commitment to advancing social reform through public education.

In their quest to secure a social agenda for the school, many
progressives, especially those siding with the pragmatic instrumentalism of Dewey, spoke out forcefully on socioeconomic themes.
There was, for instance, a ringing condemnation of any effort to
identify schooling with narrow nationalistic, social, or economic
pressures. Dewey, Childs, Counts, Bode, Newlon, Rugg, and others
were clear in describing the forces of industry and business as decidedly antagonistic to democratic and social ideals and were
roundly critical of the economic arguments used to justify social-
efficiency approaches to curriculum making. These same progressives were also prominent critics of the idea that class division was
biologically grounded in human nature and were united in castigat-
ing the tendency toward laissez-faire individualism in the industrial
and financial sectors of society. The effect was a widened sense of
purpose for the school that included more than academic prowess
or economic gain and that, as mentioned, marked a movement toward a more universal, publicly supported school system.

While much of progressivism was clearly not lukewarm to socioeconomic causes, neither was it inclined toward revolutionary or
radical social change. The "unradical" character of the early progressive tradition might explain why there is so little willingness to
appreciate its socioeconomic analysis. Progressive-experimentalists
such as Dewey and Bode believed that the relation between social
class and school was of great importance, but they flatly rejected
the idea that class struggle was essential to the improvement of soci-

ety. They believed that the conditions of industrialism required a school system that would educate the rising generation of youth with the tools of thinking and problem-solving, not with ideological passions for specific programs of social reform (although Counts and Childs did support this latter focus within the context of inquiry and debate).

Social Planning and Social Criticism

The social-class analysis of the progressive tradition is probably best characterized by the important work of Counts, especially prior to his well-known book, *Dare the Schools Build a New Social Order?* (1932). Counts' views in his most famous work were very much grounded in the statistical research he conducted during the 1920s; *Dare the Schools . . .* was, in effect, the philosophical expression of Counts' earlier scholarly efforts in social science, reinforcing his early message that the goals of democracy and educational opportunity in American public schools were still largely unfulfilled. Although Counts was somewhat removed from the spirit of experimentalism, he was trained as a social scientist and stated his case against the school—particularly in works such as *The Selective Character of American Secondary Education* (1922), *School and Society in Chicago* (1928), and *The Social Composition of Boards of Education* (1927)—with a factual and dispassionate account of the socioeconomic disparities that the school had had a hand in perpetuating. "In a very large measure," wrote Counts (1922), "participation in the privileges of a secondary education is contingent on social and economic status" (p. 149). Counts showed that socioeconomic factors had influenced various levels of school organization. He observed, for instance, that the membership of school boards was drawn from favored socioeconomic classes that had little interest in drafting educational policy that altered the status quo (Counts, 1927). Elsewhere, he hammered at the point of inequity and economic injustice by indicating that high school dropouts included disproportionate numbers of the poor, despite the fact that, at least among those who were in school, there was no evidence of inferiority among these children. In the end, Counts (1922) concluded that high school education was "a privilege being extended at public expense to those very classes that already occupy the privileged positions in modern society" (p. 152).

Counts was challenged by Charters (Gutek, 1984), who acknowledged class influence in the school but refused to accept it as necessarily negative or oppressive. According to Charters, Counts failed to show any substantive association between the nature of educational policy that was supposedly in thrall to class interests and the actual nature of the class interests of those in power, particularly those on school boards. It was entirely possible, contended Charters, that elected or appointed school board members could work in the interests of the greatest common good rather than in the interests of their own class. Charters indicated quite properly that Counts' position may have involved overgeneralization. However, Counts' statistical arguments (and later his rhetorical prose) about the role of socioeconomic class in schooling led many to rethink their views of the school's mission in relation to the socioeconomic situation.

For Counts, the problem with schooling had less to do with the institution of school itself than with the larger socioeconomic situation, which he described as an economic aristocracy. Without the reconstruction of the economic order, the school would always be a handmaiden to those who possessed economic power. On this point, Counts projected his worst fears, stating that the maintenance of an economic elite would lead to differential forms of education constructed along class lines. In the resulting dual system, the children of the masses would attend inferior schools suited for their presumed subordinate status. To avoid these perils, Counts reasoned that the schools would need to deliberately resist the domination of the economic aristocracy by revitalizing collectivist democratic causes and principles in the school. Since the controlling hand of economic oppression infused the school with the philosophy of economic individualism, which fostered egoistic and competitive values in education, the schools themselves, particularly the teachers, would need to defuse this power by committing themselves to reordering the socioeconomic order in the direction of a collectivist or workers' society. This kind of preset commitment to a social arrangement put Counts on the periphery of experimentalism; but it is not easy to dismiss him because, within the collectivist context, he did believe in the need for students to confront problematic situations in ways that developed their reflective powers. In fact, Childs (1956) and Callahan (1971) have argued that Counts was a pragmatist in the Deweyan tradition.

The problem that Counts highlighted led to a progressive call to involve the school more directly in the social and economic affairs of democracy by using it as an instrument for social planning. This has been interpreted by some to mean that the progressives had an ideal and specific sense of a society that, once erected, would simply seek to adjust individuals to its conditions. Counts, of course, fell into this conceptual trap when he tried to use the school to impose the "good indoctrination" of democracy upon youth. The irony here is that Counts opened himself up to this type of criticism by taking the radical stance of rejecting neutrality and embracing ideology in the educational program. Thus, paradoxically, it was Counts' radicalism (for instance, his belief in using the school to directly recast the economy of the nation) that elicited accusations of indoctrination and social planning.

This very same problem erupted when Childs argued along the same lines, calling for education to assume a "definite responsibility for sharing in the development of certain new ideological patterns" aimed at reforming the industrial order. "Under present socio-economic conditions," stated Childs, "it seems to me that the only adequate social point of view for education is one which includes as an essential part the conception of class struggle" (quoted in Bode, 1938a, p. 38). Bode (1938a) attacked this notion by arguing that if the social ideal of schooling turned toward class struggle, the society would be in position of using the school to support a doctrinaire viewpoint. Using a tactic that resonates with current discussions about politically correct thinking, Bode (1938a) observed that "apparently we are being told that 'imposition' is not really a crime but a high moral obligation, provided, of course, that it is of the right kind and done in the right way" (p. 39). Bode argued that what Childs proposed was not education at all, but conditioning toward a particular programmatic position that equated democracy with "a specific scheme of ownership and distribution" (p. 39). These were severe violations to Bode, who believed that the supreme ground for democracy was a scientific and moral one, in which conclusions about the social order or any other manner could not be predetermined. Bode (1935a) also insisted that the economic reconstruction of society through the school was misguided because it limited the ideal of reconstruction to one facet of life and perverted the entire process of reconstruction with a prior commitment to democratic collectivism. According to Bode, the processes of reconstruction in the school experience had to be directed at all the basic patterns of life. The character of this reconstruction, however, could never be known beforehand.

Counts (1935) and later Childs (1938) responded to Bode with an unabashed defense of the primacy of economic conditions to all of life and with the contention that economic reconstruction was at

the very heart of the broader reform and transformation of the society. Thus the lines were drawn for a debate that questioned the extent to which ideological premises could be used to direct reform
in a reconstructive learning strategy.

True to form, Dewey (1938a) entered the debate and based his
position on the idea of free and scientific inquiry, stating that as
long as the conclusions about the social planning of economic institutions were derived from a method of investigation and cooperative discussion, there would be nothing undemocratic about it.
Dewey (1938a) also said that the belief that there was a need to
exercise more control and planning in the economic affairs of the
society did not constitute a specific ideological position, but rather
a point for inquiry and debate. Writing together, Dewey and Childs
(1933) made it clear that the role of social planning was an essential
part of an education built on experimental inquiry. The idea was
not to use the school to implement a societal plan that was final and
complete, but rather to use the school in a manner that would put
students in touch with social exigencies and experimental inquiry
processes that served the broader aim of social planning:

> There is a difference between a society which is planned and a society
> which is continuously planning—namely, the difference between au-
> tocracy and democracy, between dogma and intelligence in operation,
> between suppression of individuality and that release and utilization
> of individuality which will bring it to full maturity. (p. 72)

To Counts and Childs, no definition of democracy could be considered adequate unless it included recognition of the need to reconstruct the economic system. Such a reconstruction, however,
had to be experimentally developed. Childs saw no problem with
using the economic problems of the day, as they related to reforms
supporting a workers' society, as the starting points for inquiry,
while Bode supported broad areas of conflict in our cultural heritage as appropriate starting points. Despite differences in method,
leading progressive educators were united in advocating the use of
the school to build a better and more just society, especially as related to the basic social and economic order.

The premium put on planning underscored the progressive-
experimentalist aversion to single or final plans, a position that is
contrary to the radical claim that progressives sought to adjust
youth to a unified sense of social harmony. Bobbitt and Charters, it
should be recalled, did believe that education could be used as a

conforming mechanism that adjusted individuals to their world. These social-efficiency concerns, coupled with the forthright manner in which Counts supported the idea of indoctrinating youth with a particular ideological viewpoint, helped to contribute to the notion that progressives stood for planned social control working in the interests of planned social harmony. Early interest in the social-efficiency practices can even be found in the work of Rugg, whose later commitment to the experimentalist tradition is clear. But as explained, such a position on a planned society was contrary to the experimentalism of Dewey and those progressives who worked in his shadow. Given his experience in examining schools of totalitarian societies, Dewey was well versed in the effort to control educative processes through fixed and determined societal ends. He saw that such a belief had adherents from a wide ideological spectrum. "The disciples of Lenin and Mussolini," observed Dewey, "vie with the captains of capitalistic society in endeavoring to bring about a formation of dispositions and ideas which will conduce to a preconceived goal" (1927, p. 200). It is indeed interesting that Dewey should stand accused of the same crime.

It should also be noted that during the early 1930s, Counts' *Dare the Schools Build a New Social Order?* helped create a perspective on teaching that was clearly concerned with socioeconomic factors. As expressed in *A Call to the Teachers of the Nation* (Committee of the Progressive Association on Social and Economic Problems, 1933), this new approach to teaching called on teachers to recognize their social obligation to build a better social order. The bold language in the report, which was written by a committee that included, among others, George Counts, Jesse Newlon, Merle Curti, and Sidney Hook, made it clear that socioeconomic concerns were at the forefront of progressive thought. The report maintained that, to build a better social order and to extricate themselves from undue economic and political interest, teachers

will have to emancipate themselves completely from the dominance of the business interests of the nation, cease cultivating the manners and associations of bankers and promotion agents, repudiate utterly the ideal of material success as the goal of education, abandon the smug middle-class tradition on which they have been nourished in the past, acquire a realistic understanding of the forces that actually rule the world, and formulate a fundamental program of thought and action that will deal honestly and intelligently with the problems of industrial civilization. (p. 20)

These are hardly the kinds of characteristics one might expect from educators serving the status quo.

It is important to underscore the fact that although the social-class analysis provided by prominent progressives was strongly worded and vital, it was not, except perhaps for Counts, charged with ideological rhetoric about waging a political and class war and engaging in so-called strategies of counterhegemony. Dewey himself quipped that it would be revolution enough if educators recognized social change and acted on that recognition in the schools. However, even Counts, who offered passionate statements about using the school to reform the economic order, worked within the institutionalized structure of public education and opted for experimentalist procedures of reflection and problem-focused inquiry in the school, although in a frame of reference that espoused ideologically determined conclusions. The question was whether this so-called frame of reference was actually political doctrine.

To the experimentalists, learning could not be democratic and intelligent if it was encumbered with the mission of imposing and inculcating particular ideological viewpoints. This did not mean that schooling had to be neutral; it did mean, however, that the methods used to deal with socioeconomic concerns in the schools had to be those of investigation and cooperative discussion. In fact, the dangers of neutrality in the curriculum were outlined by several progressives who used an argument that has since been adopted by radicals. For example, Newlon (1939a), who has been criticized for his commitment to social control and the dominance of managerial prerogatives in the curriculum, minced few words in stating:

> Neither the school nor the teaching profession can ever maintain a neutral position with reference to critical social problems. The influences seeking to maintain the economic status-quo could ask nothing more of the school and of the teachers than that they should attempt a role of neutrality. (p. 263)

Since progressive-experimentalists articulated an educational theory to accompany their social theory, they widened their argumentation about schooling in areas pertaining to curricular method and to the advancement of social causes through the school. Unfortunately, this also tempted the charge of an *a priori* instrumentalism and the advocacy of adjustment education to a predesigned sense of social harmony. It is true, however, that progressives such as Dewey, Childs, and Bode opted to use the school in a manner that would cultivate the spirit of experimental inquiry for the purpose of social planning. This idea of planning, as indicated, was seen as ongoing experimental activity that was evolutionary rather than revolutionary in its effects.

Ironically, the progressive focus on the practical is precisely what current curriculum radicals have ignored and, in some cases, disparaged. Interestingly, this seems to be changing with the growing recognition of theoretical isolationism in the radical discourse. Giroux and Aronowitz (1985), for instance, have noted that the scholarship inspired by critical theory has a pessimistic character that tends to default on the commitment to curricular possibilities and the development of schools as sites for individual and collective empowerment. Elsewhere, Giroux (1984) exclaimed that "radicals need to develop theories of practice rather than theories for practice" (p. 129). This understanding, coupled with the global political demise of Marxism, might explain why Dewey, whose ideas on the curriculum merged theory with practice, is undergoing a kind of rehabilitation in radical discourse.

The recourse to practice among radicals, however, is more closely aligned with Counts than with Dewey, since many contemporary radicals put forth a social theory that assumes a goodness of fit between their ideology and the needs of the society. A good deal of friction occurs even with Counts, however, since he opted for the scientific method as the main method of intellectual pursuit, although, as mentioned, within a firmly staked-out ideological position.

Nonradical Analysis

The contemporary dissatisfaction with the work of many early progressives in the area of social-class analysis, then, has likely had much to do with their decidedly un-Marxist solution to the problem of class division. Ravitch (1977), of course, made this point in her critique of the radical revisionist historians, showing that much of the criticism made against progressive thought was simply driven by the belief that the movement was not radical enough. Such a criticism against progressives is acceptable if it is not accompanied by a distortion of the historical record. In the case of Dewey, for example, one could argue that he might have left us with a different and a more valuable legacy had he been more radical, but one cannot legitimately argue that he ignored issues pertaining to the relation between the school and the economic order, or that he somehow, through his belief in the common school, supported the status quo and an education of life adjustment.

Altogether, the progressive-experimentalists were not very responsive to Marxist thought. Dewey's hostility toward what might today be called orthodox Marxism, for example, was fairly well established; in *Freedom and Culture* (1939) he cited its failure to place its own "generalizations in their office of working hypotheses" and accused it of embracing a "monistic block-universe theory of social causation" (pp. 71, 72). Unlike most radical critics today, who generally avoid examining schooling in Marxist societies, Dewey (and also Counts) worked first-hand in such places. Even Counts, who was attacked by media figures for supposedly espousing a Marxist interpretation of education and for urging the schools to sow the seeds for the eventual triumph of a classless society, never claimed to be Marxist and offered much criticism of Marxism, especially as it existed in the Soviet state. It should be stressed that, despite his class-conscious language, Counts did not embrace the material dialectic of Marx in his commentary, opting instead for an experimentalist procedure. He posed his solution to the class divisions in society in terms of a unified cultural unit devoted to democracy, an abhorrent result from the critical theory perspective, but one that did not compromise the veracity of his social-class analysis.

SUMMARY

The progressive movement in American education comprises a broad conceptual territory. In terms of the curriculum field, however, the meliorist tradition represented by Dewey and other experimentalists has made considerable progress in constructing a working framework for curriculum development. There is a long heritage of thought that has helped to weave the factors of the learner, the society, and the subject matter into the fabric of curriculum theory and development. The evolution of thinking about these factors has occurred within the framework of the original principles articulated by American pragmatists, who sought to identify behavior as the central unit of analysis for philosophy and who aimed to use the reconstruction of present experience, guided by the scientific method, as the wellspring for the improvement of life conditions. Despite radical commentary to the contrary, the problem-focused basis of this perspective and its democratic value orientation have led many progressive-experimentalists to engage in a spirited and sweeping socioeconomic analysis of the school and the society. Dewey, in fact, used his own class analysis to underscore the need for the school to address societal differences in ways that led to elevated levels of social tolerance and social understanding. He synthesized a method of intelligence (reflective or scientific thought) with a worldview of democracy and helped shape an enduring, albeit underimplemented, framework for curriculum policy and practice.

CHAPTER 5

THE CRISIS OF DESIGN

> It is the office of the school to balance the varied elements in the social environment, and to see to it that each individual gets the opportunity to escape from the limitations of the social group in which he was born and to come into contact with a broader environment.
>
> John Dewey

Curriculum development issues have always been central to educational policy discussions. During the past decade, curriculum considerations have taken center stage in discussions about the formulation of national curriculum standards and the establishment of alternative "schools of choice." Questions have been raised about whether the public school should serve some overarching civic and cultural purpose or whether individualistic and more parochial concerns should take precedence in the curriculum. Unfortunately, these questions have been framed in dichotomous terms. As a result, the common school and the common curriculum have come under attack as unsympathetic to the diversities of our society, leading inevitably to the widespread call for the dissolution of the common school in favor of schools based on community or family dictates.

This call has been made with equal conviction from both conservative and radical ranks. Certain conservative forces, for instance, have reasserted their desire to have the school operate under the conditions of marketplace economics, while radical forces, ever critical of the oppressive character of public schooling, have appropriated the very same idea (although with certain regulatory safeguards added). The result has been the opening of the floodgates on alternative curriculum design ideas, as the belief in school variety and choice for the sake of variety and choice has grown in popularity.

As Barrow (1976) put it, the designing of a curriculum is tantamount to defining education itself. As illustrated in the previous chapters, progressive-experimentalists gave life to their theoretical ideas in the actual development of the school curriculum. Many radicals, however, have been unable to support a method or approach to curriculum planning, instead supporting the idea of school alternativeness; essentially, this has meant advocating, within certain limits, a wide range of alternatives because of the contribution they collectively make to the cause of diversity and to the development of self-determined community schools.

It is precisely on this point that the intersection of certain conservative and radical positions becomes clear. The idea of educational variety, for instance, which many radicals see as breaking the imperialistic back of the public school, is very similar to the economic conservative premise of competitive individualism in a free market. Similarly, the belief in community-controlled schools, which to many radicals represents an opportunity for schools (particularly city schools) to recognize local ethnic and cultural traditions, is a tenet of cultural conservativism, in which the principle of self-determination is held to be a primary right of the cultural group. In these circumstances, the individual could become subjected to community-based pressures that reinforce the consensual and traditional (Bowers, 1987). Thus the shibboleths of "variety" and "choice" are proclaimed by an odd alliance of economic conservatives, cultural conservatives, and radicals working out of the critical theory literature.

Under the current decentralized system of schooling, the common schools of America are designed to be responsive to community concerns, but in a manner that transcends the parochial lines of family and community. It should be emphasized that such an arrangement is unique to the United States and is deliberately antinational; it seeks to protect the school from the influence of nationally driven special interests. The common school, in this sense, is only common to the degree that it attends to broad societal values and aims. Moreover, a progressive vision of the common school, which was embodied in the *Cardinal Principles* report (Commission for the Reorganization of Secondary Education, 1918), holds to a comprehensive view of the curriculum and to the understanding that the school must fulfill academic, social, vocational, and personal educational agendas; it is a site not only for general education (common learnings) but also for specialized, exploratory, and enrichment education.

Confusion about the role of the common school has led to overall confusion about the direction of public schooling in America.

Clearly, the way out of the educational confusion is not to embrace a uniformly reductive model of curriculum development, as Hirsch (1987) and other conservative essentialists have maintained, but to find a broad basis for the development of a school curriculum that is at once directive and flexible. I will argue that this can best be accomplished by recovering the pragmatism inherent in the progressive curriculum literature.

As will be explained, an initial step in reinstating the pragmatic tradition in curriculum design is to recover the lost function of general education in the curriculum and to reexamine the process of curriculum development as a way to create learning experiences that blend a scientific way of thought with a democratic way of life. This is, in a manner of speaking, an education appropriate for all youth. Such an educational outlook is vital to the maintenance of public schools in which all groups in our society can interact in fellowship and to the development of those understandings and appreciations that form the basis of our unity in diversity.

THE UNEASY ALLIANCE: IDEOLOGIES OF CHOICE IN SCHOOL REFORM

A number of critics have recently alleged that the organizational and financial structure of public education hinders any opportunity for innovative and alternative school development. Conservative economic critics, for instance, have contended that public schooling in America operates as a kind of monopoly that generates complacency and stagnancy (Friedman & Friedman, 1980; Kearns & Doyle, 1988), while radical critics have argued along similar lines, maintaining that the public school exercises a cultural monopoly and social control over the student population, thus institutionalizing the inequitable treatment of underclass youth (Anyon, 1981; Apple, 1979; Bowles & Gintis, 1976; Coons & Sugarman, 1978).

Such criticisms have naturally given rise to renewed discussion about ways to broaden school programs and increase parental involvement in school decision making. The last decade alone has witnessed increasing efforts to groom public support for policies that give parents wider latitude in choosing their children's schools. This has been treated in both the professional literature and the popular press as a structural reform that could potentially invigorate new levels of responsiveness, variety, and flexibility in all schools (public and private). However, such a movement raises profound questions about the role and responsibility of public education. It represents a defining moment for the progressive hope of common public schooling dedicated to the democratization of society and amelioration of social ills.

Increasingly, the premium placed on choice is leading to the fragmentation of the school into networks of widely disparate alternative schools. According to Raywid (1984), the scope of the alternative school offerings range "from relatively free schools to fundamentalist types, with even a military academy or two" (p. 72). In these alternative schools, the curriculum is expressly concerned with the individualistic instructional needs of the learner; it embodies no wider social agenda. Thus, for one learner, a school that features skill-drill approaches might be valued because it provides needed security and structure; for another, a school that stresses experiential learning might be attractive because it serves the goals of personal and social inquiry; for yet another, a school that provides a particular ethnic stamp might be perceived to be most appropriate. In this way, alternative schools of choice can claim that they are breaking away from a narrow tradition that sees one best way of educating all youngsters.

All this has had a disruptive effect on the progressive belief in the sociocivic function of public schooling. While progressive-experimentalists have maintained the belief that the public school should civilize the society by transmitting our human heritage and by instilling the dispositions needed to transform this heritage into new insight, the idea of school choice has driven a wedge between schooling deemed to be appropriate for and by the family, and schooling deemed to be appropriate for and by the wider society. There are, of course, differences between the kinds of choice mechanisms that conservatives and radicals prefer, but the common effect has been to slam the door on the progressive effort to fashion a common and comprehensive public school devoted to the fulfillment of a broad sociocivic mission. The culpability of the radicals in this affair is clear. As Bowers (1991a, 1991b) observed, the negativity of critical theory encourages a continuing clash of ideas that relativizes and ultimately subverts our commonalities and sense of interdependence. In criticizing Giroux and McLaren, Bowers (1991b) explained that "there is no recognition that human beings are part of a larger set of information and energy nets" (p. 482). This problem is exemplified in the school choice argument, in which various types of conservatives and radicals take an axe to the main root of common schooling and the provision of a common universe of discourse, understanding, and competence.

In the United States, the first systematic effort to develop a plan for school choice mechanisms was articulated by the economist Milton Friedman (1962). He was among the first to cast a dissenting vote against the then-popular trend toward national uniformity in the schools. It should be recalled that during the mid-to-late 1950s and the early 1960s few questioned the character and extent of governmental responsibility in the affairs of the public schools. Given the space race, the school was resolutely dedicated to meeting narrow nationalistic needs. The educational leadership fell in line with this overarching priority and helped to develop educational policies committed to securing nationally consolidated educational outcomes.

Friedman, however, believed that the ultimate source of school control should be the individual consumer (the parent). In seeking to develop a framework whereby to secure this goal, Friedman advanced the now-familiar argument for "schools of choice." American education, he claimed, could best be improved by changing the financial and governance structure of public education in directions that encouraged schools to compete for students and that helped parents exercise consumer choice in deciding where their children would be educated. The idea was straightforward: Provide parents with redeemable vouchers (which are roughly equivalent to the per-pupil expenditures of the local school) and permit them to spend their vouchers at schools of their choice. Friedman advocated no substantive restrictions on the participating "voucher" schools, stating that each school need only be approved by the government much in the way, to use his analogy, that the government inspects restaurants to ensure minimum sanitary standards. Interestingly, given Freidman's argument, one could say that the effort by conservatives to destabilize the public school challenged the radical assumption that schools reproduce the status quo.

Friedman's proposal, however, turned out to be an educational nonevent. Part of the problem was the tenor of the times, which, as mentioned, was inhospitable to his call for the diffusion of the government's responsibilities in the operation of the public school. With the space race in full gear, American education was in a state of national mobilization. Major curriculum projects, rich in monies authorized by the National Science Foundation, came onto the national scene and influenced classroom instruction in the general education phases of the curriculum (Tanner & Tanner, 1980). This was especially true at the secondary school level. The focus of the curriculum was on the cultivation of the intellectual powers of youth through highly discipline-centered studies in subjects important to the nation's defense, such as mathematics, physics, chemistry, and foreign language (Goodlad, 1966; Tanner & Tanner, 1980). The curriculum was a monolith built according to a compelling nationalistic impulse, and any proposal that distracted the school from this central objective was characteristically met with disapproval from local school authorities. Even the procedure of curriculum planning, which had been the sacrosanct province of the educator, was forfeited to "scholar-specialists" (physicists, mathematicians, and historians) who were presumably better able to ensure the integrity of each vital subject area in the traditional curriculum.

By most accounting, Friedman's proposal for school choice was little more than an economist's attempt to impose the principles of a free-market economy on the schools, but the rhetoric supporting these changes was often colored with a strong sociocivic sentiment that spoke to broader matters such as equality of educational opportunity for all youth and empowerment for low-income parents. These themes would later be captured by radical commentators, who would find themselves in the unusual position of favoring the spirit of capitalism's most cherished principle—competitive marketing with limited restrictions—as it was justified in various education voucher plans. Friedman had, in effect, stolen a line from the radical rhetoric by claiming that access to good public schooling was circumscribed by enrollment policies patterned according to highly stratified residential zones. He maintained that this had the effect of restricting the intermingling of youth from different backgrounds and thwarting the opportunity of low-income parents to exercise intelligent choice over where their children went to school. School choice, then, was a matter of social justice because in the absence of the financial resources needed to send their children to a private school or to move into a more expensive neighborhood, low-income parents were forced to send their children to schools that were often debilitated with social and pedagogical problems.

During the 1960s, the school continued to be attacked as a monopolistic institution by an army of radical romantics. The major figures of the emerging New Left in American education included A. S. Neill (in England), John Holt, Jonathan Kozol, George Dennison, Herbert Kohl, Paul Goodman, Edgar Friedenberg, and Ivan Illich. Originating in literary circles, this radical–romantic group presented its message in bitter tones of social protest and social criticism. Altogether, they maintained a deep hostility and mistrust toward what they viewed as a grim educational establishment. Goodman's work exemplified this general conviction. In 1964, he wrote:

> In the tender grades, the schools are a babysitting service during a period of collapse of the old-type family and during a time of extreme urbanization and urban mobility. In the junior and senior high school grades, they are an arm of the police, providing cops and concentration camps paid for under the heading "Board of Education." (p. 22)

The titles of the books and articles that were published by the radical-romantic element emphasized the dehumanizing and iniquitous nature of the educational establishment. Consider the following titles: Kozol's *Death at an Early Age: The Destruction of the Hearts and Minds of Negro Children in the Boston Public Schools* (1967), Goodman's *Compulsory Mis-Education* (1964), and Nat Hentoff's *Our Children Are Dying* (1966). As a literary phenomenon, the writings emerging from the radical-romantic camp were little more than remonstrations about an educational system that had supposedly lost its soul.

However, these radical critics also expressed a romantic compassion and maudlin faith in the self-educating forces of a free and unhampered childhood and adolescence (free from adult intervention). To one extreme faction, this meant that the school environment had to be reconstructed in order to free the child to direct his or her own education. In A. S. Neill's (1962) Summerhill school in England, for instance, the application of this notion meant that nothing resembling a curriculum existed in the school; books were renounced, teaching was viewed as interference in the growth of the child, and a wanton freedom to do as one pleased was advocated. But to other extreme elements, advocacy of an unhampered learning experience resulted in rejecting school altogether. Believing that learning is not the result of instruction but rather of unrestricted participation in society, Friedenberg, for example, opposed compulsory school attendance, adding that perhaps "bumming around the Near East" could serve as a useful alternative (quoted in Brossard, 1967, p. 75).

The protest and intemperate criticism in the writings of the radical romantics was soon translated into a nationwide appeal for alternative schools and alternative programs devoted to a humanizing mission. In little time, free schools, the open classroom, and a welter of nontraditional school approaches all came into style (Graubard, 1974). The concept of providing school choices was well suited for the mood of this period because it helped to advance the cause of educational variety and liberation from the "invidious" public school.

Another source of vitality for the "choice" concept, however, was associated with the growing perception that the schools were perpetuating rather than ameliorating class differences in our society. Even mainstream figures such as Goodlad (1976) observed that "instead of being the circuit breaker, [schooling] had become part of the system for mandating educational differences" (p. 95). Many believed that voucher programs could improve public school desegregation efforts and thereby resuscitate the school's role in facilitating economic and social mobility. And with the finding of the landmark Coleman report (Coleman et al., 1966) that school achievement among Negro youth was likely to improve if they attended schools with white youngsters from homes supportive of education (without lowering the achievement for whites), the argument for testing the desegregative powers of vouchers drew added strength. Many radicals would use this tack to support their position on vouchers, alternative schools, and tax tuition credits.

The convergence of conservative and radical rhetoric continued into the 1970s. At the level of the White House and the Office of Economic Opportunity (OEO), the Nixon administration looked upon vouchers as a way to improve education without increasing expenditures; vouchers also fell in line with the Republican mandate for less government presence in the affairs of society. In 1969, the OEO had shown enough confidence in the idea to grant Christopher Jencks three-quarters of a million dollars to study the voucher question.

Jencks' (1972a) work was quite important because it analyzed the character of different voucher approaches. Altogether he examined seven alternative voucher plans, eventually concluding that a regulated form of vouchers could hold the key to making our schools more attractive and more democratic. He also cautioned that an unregulated voucher system (such as the one espoused by Friedman) could be an extremely serious setback for the education of disadvantaged children. If nothing else, Jencks made it clear that the debate about vouchers had to be expanded to include consideration of specific voucher proposals.

Only a short time later, however, Jencks would emerge as a powerful voice against the educational viability of all public schooling. In a book entitled *Inequality*, Jencks (1972b) attempted to show how the public school had only marginal significance in developing the cognitive skills of youth and in enhancing their odds for economic mobility. Supported by a $500,000 grant from the Carnegie Corporation and carried out with the assistance of a team of Harvard researchers, the study reanalyzed the data gathered from Coleman's work (together with supplementary data taken from the U.S. Census Bureau) and emerged with conclusions that focused on the limits of schools (on what schools cannot accomplish). The central finding was that schools were not effective in equalizing incomes and that any effort to equalize educational opportunities in school would simply be wasted effort (at least in an economic sense). The study also maintained that the benefits of desegregation were so slight that minority parents should be free to choose whether their children attended segregated or desegregated schools. Lastly, the study revealed that what one brings to the school environment (family characteristics) is far more important, in terms of standardized measures of cognitive skill, than any characteristic imparted by the school. This last proposition turned out to be a virtual command for school divestiture, a policy widely favored by political conservatives.

Jencks also provided considerable ammunition to the causes of economic and cultural conservativism by espousing a rationale that justified limiting the school's role on the grounds that it failed to facilitate economic balance. Jencks, in fact, saw the problem of economic inequality as an issue that had to be solved practically at the expense of the school. "We should try to change the structure of the job market," he noted; "there is a more promising way of going at it than keeping everybody in school longer" (Jencks, 1972c, p. 257). A fairer economy in essence meant a more restricted commitment to the school. With this implication in mind, the popular press began to turn to Jencks' work to uphold the reductionist agenda of economic conservatives. *Time* magazine concluded, for instance, that "Jencks finds no reason to believe that spending more money will greatly improve the quality of schooling" ("What Schools Cannot Do," p. 41). Jencks (1972b) obliged this manner of thinking by proclaiming that the character of a school's output in the area of cognitive skill "depended largely on a single input, namely the characteristics of the entering children. Everything else—the school budget, its policies, the characteristics of the teachers—is either secondary or completely irrelevant" (p. 256). It began to look as though the school made no difference, not only from an economic standpoint but also from a cognitive one.

Interestingly, in a *Phi Delta Kappan* interview released after the publication of *Inequality*, Jencks (1972c) admitted to his bias of favoring the home as the more important educational agency and to his "inclination" to make schooling compulsory only up to age 14.

As an product of Exeter Academy and Harvard University, Jencks seemed to be advocating a retreat from education "for other people's children" (Tanner, 1974). This was a concern made clear by ten prominent black sociologists and educators in a collective opinion published in the *Harvard Educational Review* (Edmonds et al., 1973). They opined that "the reaction of the press and the public to Jencks' study suggests that many people are looking for arguments which will free them of the responsibility to provide quality education for all children" (p. 89).

This charge would also be made against those who supported the deschooling of society, most prominently Ivan Illich, Everett Reimers, and Paul Goodman. Havighurst (1971), for example, asserted that without free public schools, the division between the wealthy and the poor could only be exacerbated, since the well-to-do would always be able to purchase the most and the best in a free-market system of education. Conservative themes were palpable in this context. The proposed effort to widen and alter the sites for public education not only had a toehold in economic conservativism, but it also provided the leeway needed for the local expression of cultural conservatism in school development.

During this period many radicals continued to walk hand in hand with various conservatives through their support for tuition credits. This position was prominent in the anarchistic commentary of Ivan Illich. Arguing the need to deschool society, Illich (1971) wanted to replace the institution of schooling with access to an "edu-credit card" that would allow individuals to receive an education wherever and whenever they might find it. Reimers (1971) also supported the idea of providing personal educational allowances for individuals to use throughout life as they purchase their education from sundry "educational" sources in the society. In doing so, both Illich and Reimers proposed an idea with an even stronger free-market ideal than Milton Friedman's proposal. As indicated, in each case, it was the obliteration of the common public school that was the desired effect. The question of what knowledge was most worthwhile in the education of citizens was left to the quixotic adjustment between the buyers and sellers in the educational marketplace.

During the mid-1970s sociopolitical conditions resulted in a widespread feeling that too many educational dollars had been spent in previous reform periods and that cutbacks were now in order. Conservative and radical mandates, however, continued to overlap. Acting under the pressure of tighter budgets, school administrators throughout the country turned to an old educational standby: the "no-frills" skill-development model of fundamental, or basic-skills, education. Vouchers and other choice proposals became less popular, but at the secondary education level, the growing mood of educational retrenchment found an unlikely partner in the idea of alternative schools. As it turned out, several national commission reports stressed the need for the institution of schooling to look for alternative ways to educate adolescents (National Commission on the Reform of Secondary Education, 1973; National Panel on High School and Adolescent Education, 1976; Panel on Youth of the President's Science Advisory Committee, 1974). The idea of alternative schools was now put directly in the service of fulfilling the goals of economic conservatives. Much of the discussion in these forums, for instance, centered around the need to offer students the option of entering into alternative work-training arrangements. To facilitate this process, the commissions advocated dropping the school-leaving age to 14, reducing the length of the school day, and diminishing the role of the curriculum in students' school experience (less time in school obviously meant less time to provide students with a broad education). The idea was to break the monopoly of the school not through vouchers but through the proliferation of other "educative" institutions (mostly business- or work-related), an idea that resonated with Illich's effort to transfer the control of schooling to various segments of the society. The reductionist recommendations offered by the commissions turned out to be a way of supporting the liberation of youth from the tentacles of the public school, which was still being portrayed as a stultifying monolith. The commissions, in effect, called for the broadening of education through the concomitant narrowing of the school's educative responsibilities. The competitive individualism of the marketplace was as much a source of emancipation to the conservative critics as cultural and psychic individualism was to critical theorists.

With the approach of the 1980s, the voucher proposal had come full circle, as economic conservatives argued for a free school marketplace. Spokespersons in the Department of Education enthusiastically supported vouchers because they felt that the guiding conception of parental sovereignty in a competitive climate would improve the school's responsiveness and accountability. William Bennett, then Secretary of Education, was particularly active in his support, prominently displaying "choice" as one of the main conceptual threads of his administration. Later Bennett (1987) contradicted his support for choice by also supporting the philosophically conservative idea of framing an academic secondary school curriculum, built on the literary–humanist traditions of Western civilization, for the education of all youth.

The most recent development in the school choice movement has centered around the release of John Chubb and Terry Moe's *Politics, Markets and America's Schools* (1990), a book that makes an empirical case for the dissolution of state control of the public school in favor of widespread privitization. Chubb and Moe's belief that modern public schools are structurally inhospitable to the release of teacher intelligence and to the overall development of educative learning experiences is a conceptual premise shared by most radicals, who have long maintained that schools are institutions of social control. The Marxist-inspired case made by Bowles and Gintis (1976) for reproduction theory in the public schools is based exactly on this contention. Little wonder, then, that the exercise of free-market choices in the context of the schools has been proudly perceived by its own conservative adherents as a radical initiative. Chester Finn (1991), the politically conservative ideologue for educational policy in the Bush administration, has recently begun to refer to himself as a "revolutionary"; he has even embraced the symbolic language of democratization efforts in Russia (*perestroika,* which literally means "reconstruction") as part of his school improvement rhetoric. The irony in all of this is that economic conservatives, who currently cite the need for more diversity and variety in schools, seem, on the point of "school choice," to be more strongly allied with radicals than with fellow philosophical conservatives, such as Theodore Sizer, Mortimer Adler, and even William Bennett, who argued during the 1980s that schooling in America was too diverse, too fragmented, and literally too comprehensive. It should be recalled that reformers such as Sizer (1984) and Adler (1982) argued for a "less is more" mentality in curriculum reform and sought to build the American high school on a strict academic foundation.

Ironically, where efforts have been made to implement a network of alternative schools, the results have not always been attuned to egalitarian causes. In many school districts offering alternative "magnet school" options, for instance, a duality of quality exists between the magnet school and the conventional school. The Chicago Panel on Public School Policy and Finance, for example, stated that the city's magnet schools were allotted two more teachers than nonmagnet schools of comparable size, received additional monies through federal grants, and had smaller class sizes. The executive director of the Chicago panel called the magnet program "a whole system of elite schools" ("Magnet Schools," 1987). Magnet schools have generated a problem known as "skimming," a process whereby the brightest and most motivated students are "skimmed" from their respective neighborhood schools, thereby contributing to the deterioration of the local public school. This problem has also been documented by Moore and Davenport (1990) as it applied to magnet schools in the New York, Boston, Chicago, and Philadelphia school districts. They referred to school choice schemes as "new forms of segregation" that exacerbate and legitimatize the inequities in schooling.

The shifting nature of support for alternative schools and the accompanying proposals for vouchers, tax tuition credits, and public schools of choice have been based on the belief that the common school is an outdated institution that eschews innovation and change and that prevents diverse cultural and individualistic experiences. Alternative school options have come and gone, all justified by different ideological positions, but the erosion of support for the common public school has been steady. Radicals, wanting to escape from the cultural imperialism of public schooling, have been unwittingly advancing the privatization of public schooling and the termination of a common school working in the interests of a common democracy. Leftists, such as Giroux (1992), may currently bemoan the dangerous effects of "choice" in terms of its failure to establish diversity within the schools and to revitalize neighborhood schools in the interests of democracy, but these same radicals have not acknowledged the linkage that their own commentary has had with such effects. After characterizing the school as a sinister monolith, radicals now encounter the crisis in their own criticism and contemplate the prospect of the school's liberation in the face of marketplace imperatives. Advocacy for community control, for school variety, for parental rights, for the empowerment of the poor, and most significantly, for the exorcism of state control from the public schools, all themes once belonging to the Left, have been usurped by economic conservatives who have appealed to the logic of competition and marketplace consumerism in school policy.

RECOVERING PRAGMATISM: CURRICULUM DESIGN AND DEMOCRACY

In the Eighty-seventh Yearbook of the National Society of the Study of Education, *Critical Issues in Curriculum*, Herbert Kliebard (1988) lamented the fads and fashions that have come to represent curriculum reform in American education. In accounting for this unhealthy phenomenon, he pointed to several factors, including the problem that arises when neither limits nor any pervading conceptions of what is and is not educationally desirable are imposed on the curriculum. Referring to the curriculum he wrote, "for all intents and purposes, anything goes, and the sheer inclusiveness of what passes for the curriculum in modern times may have a great deal to do with its apparent instability" (Kliebard, 1988, p. 20). He went on to recommend that a clearer conception of schooling be developed and used "as a filter to screen out trivial or chimerical proposals for curriculum change as well as those that are best assayed in another setting. . . . Without disciplined attention to what should be excluded from the curriculum, a revolving door in curriculum matters becomes almost inevitable" (p. 20).

Clearly, the school reform cannot uncritically absorb every school claim that carries the imprimatur of "alternativeness." When school leaders maintain that every wide-ranging alternative has its place, the school is exonerated from accountability to central principles of curriculum development. The formulation of curricular policy and practice is not properly a process of styling learning according to the gut-level needs of parents and students.

The following ideas are offered in the interests of contributing to a framework of design for the American school curriculum, one that is drawn from the pragmatic movement in curriculum. Since these ideas allow for particularity and for the exercise of certain local prerogatives, they also represent potential points of agreement in the curriculum theory community.

Unity in Diversity: The Lost Function of General Education

Among the lost functions of curriculum design that could lend some stability and direction to the common school experience in America is the idea of general education. In examining the educational purpose of the comprehensive school, Maurice Holt (1978) observed that "a lingering obsession with its function as a differentiating rather than unifying institution has obscured the need to think hard about what such schools are for" (p. 38). Although, as indicated, the comprehensive common school has been berated for its use of differentiating mechanisms (such as instructional tracks and ability groups), very little has been said of its unifying function, which derives from the general education component of the school curriculum. And where its unifying component *has* been acknowledged, criticism has been directed to the manner in which the cultural sensibilities of students have been violated through the imposition of Eurocentric cultural perspectives. Thus both the specializing and the unifying elements in the curriculum of the comprehensive school have been perceived to be oppressive.

General education can be defined as "that part of the student's whole education which looks first of all to his life as a responsible human being and citizen" (Harvard Committee, 1945, p. 51). At the secondary school level, general education is equated with the common learning phase of the curriculum; its main purpose is to engage youth in a common universe of discourse, understanding, and competence that promotes the development of socially responsible citizens (Tanner & Tanner, 1980). The notion of citizenship is central to defining the curriculum character of general education; without it, general education tends to be defined generically as a common core of knowledge, skills, and values, a definition that fails to draw attention to basic curricular concerns, such as what knowledge is most worthwhile and what aims and objectives are best suited for the schools of a democracy.

General education is a curricular function that represents various pedagogical priorities. As the facet of the curriculum that deals with the knowledge that all citizens must share, general education necessitates an outlook on knowledge and teaching that is principally different from the one employed in specialized or college preparatory settings. Thus, general education is more than a function of the curriculum; it is also an orientation to learning and to curriculum design. Though it takes on different forms in different school settings, general education has historically abided by a particular set of pedagogical values and principles that are anchored in an experimentalist-progressive tradition of school thought.

Generally speaking, all education justified under general education emphasizes a sociocivic content focus that promotes problem-centered inquiry and group cooperation. General education is also marked by interdisciplinary subject matter schemes, heterogeneous classroom settings, and a curricular commitment to the educability of all youth. The learner in the general education scenario is defined as an autonomously thinking, socially responsible citizen who is able to make decisions according to an intelligent method and upon whose skills the commonweal depends. In this way, general education can claim to be more than a curriculum mechanism dedicated to common learning. In a broad sense, it is a perspective on learning that emphasizes citizenship priorities and alternative (nondisciplinary) subject-matter frameworks.

Over the years, general education has come in and out of favor with the school leadership. During the progressive period following World War II, the notion of general education was held in great esteem in the educational literature. The well-known Educational Policies Commission (EPC) report, *Education for ALL American Youth* (1944), stressed the significance of general education by highlighting a comprehensive range of needs that applied to the education of all youth and by describing how these needs might be integrated into the design of the curriculum. The concept of general education advanced in the EPC report was tied to the idea of helping students develop personal and social competencies in such areas as consumer economics, family and community life, aesthetics, health, leisure, scientific understanding, ethical values, and democratic citizenship. One-third of the entire secondary school curriculum was organized along these lines, which, as provinces of general education, were justified as fundamental areas of proficiency for democratic living. General education in this tradition was concerned not with a highly specified list of information or knowledge, but with a cluster of values, understandings, and skills that could be treated in the curriculum through a variety of subject-matter approaches. The curriculum was not content-neutral, as critics have alleged, but integrated subject matter in ways that breached the traditional disciplinary lines of knowledge. These integrative approaches to organizing subject matter in general education did not conform to any single discipline or subject field, but were dedicated to the organization of knowledge according to sociocivic themes. This emphasis on citizenship competencies was a prominent theme in the progressive educational thought of the time and was supported in practical settings, including, most significantly, the curriculum framework of the various experimental schools participating in the Eight-Year Study (Giles, McCutchen, & Zechiel, 1942).

Another notable statement on general education popularized during the post–World War II period was the Harvard Committee (1945) report, *General Education in a Free Society*. The report shared a kinship with *Education for ALL American Youth* by promoting a general education program attuned to the contemporary needs of young citizens. The Harvard report, however, departed from the progressive tradition of general education by preserving an academic subject-matter curriculum (while asking teachers to provide interdisciplinary connections in their respective classrooms) and by allowing ability groups to be constituted in the general education curriculum. The preservation of the academic structure saved the Harvard report from the conservative criticism of anti-intellectualism that was directed at *Education for ALL American Youth* (Bestor, 1956). But while the Harvard report did advance English, science, mathematics, and social studies as the core focal points for general education, it also preserved the place of vocational education in the comprehensive school setting.

During the two decades following the release of the Educational Policies Commission and Harvard Committee reports, general education lost much of its support. The emergence of the Cold War and the increasing effort to use the school as an instrument in the space race curtailed the general education function of the curriculum and overemphasized the specialized function of the curriculum (which was so fundamentally tied to the nationalistic urge to produce more scientists, mathematicians, and engineers). In his well-known *The American High School Today*, Conant (1959) addressed the importance of the general education function of in the curriculum, but he argued for a subject-centered curriculum constructed according to ability groups, a proposal that seemed better suited to the nationalistic aims of the space race than to the democratizing aims of the society. By advancing general education by name, however, Conant helped to preserve the idea of the comprehensive high school and the commitment to educating all youth in one unified setting. The comprehensive high school was an organizational structure conceptually sympathetic to the function of general education.

Interestingly, over the years, several education commentators have tried to dismantle general education in the school curriculum. The well-chronicled efforts of school critics during the Cold War period, notably Bestor (1953) and Rickover (1959), to radically alter schooling in America by recasting it in the image of the dual system used in Europe is but one example. The movement to embrace wide-ranging school alternatives during the humanizing initiatives of the late 1960s (without accounting for the functions of general education, specialized education, and exploratory education) is another example. To some, even the growth of television spelled the dissolution of general education. Impressed with the disseminating qualities of television, Sizer declared in 1972 that "the need for a common school has largely passed; television has seen to that" (p. 30). In 1984, however, Sizer (1984) would emerge as a nationally recognized reformer who, among other things, advocated a one-track curriculum devoted to the education of all youth.

The 1980s provided fertile ground for the reconsideration of general education values and themes. In 1984, Goodlad used the Harvard Committee report as a prototype in recommending the reconstruction of general education in the American public school curriculum, adding vocational education to the four required subject areas originally mentioned in the Harvard Committee report but excluding it as a specialized program in the comprehensive school setting. Goodlad's regard for general education was a welcome insight to the then-emerging excellence-in-education movement of the 1980s. Unfortunately, the nationalistic flavor of the so-called excellence movement led to an emphasis on reform in the college preparatory program, and this had the effect of subordinating the role of general education in the school. Yet the early 1980s were also marked by a spate of education reform reports that focused their sights on the reformulation of a general education curriculum. Included in the reform discussion were proposals that advanced a monolithic, one-track academic curriculum (Adler, 1982; Bennett, 1987; Sizer, 1984), proposals that called for a reconceived commitment to general education minus the placement of vocational education in the comprehensive school program (Boyer, 1983; Goodlad, 1984), and proposals that recast the educational mission of the schools in language that was responsive to techno-industrial goals (National Commission on Excellence in Education, 1983; National Science Board Commission, 1983; Task Force on Education for Economic Growth, 1983). General education, in the experimentalist-progressive sense, was not served well by any of these reform statements. With the exception of Goodlad (1984) and Boyer (1983), these reports did not articulate a general education program that was attuned to the progressive ideal of problem-focused study within a sociocivic content base. As mentioned, Goodlad (1984) and Boyer (1983) did display an understanding of the fundamental issues of general education, but they both failed to support the comprehensive concept of schooling on which general education relies.

Over the past few years, general education has undergone a spurt of popularity, largely as a result of a conservative interest in using the common curriculum as a groundwork for the conveyance of "cultural literacy" (Hirsch, 1987). As explained by Hirsch, a shared base of common knowledge is essential in generating high-quality social discussion and a sense of community among citizens. Such an ideal had long been established in the progressive literature, fundamentally rooted in such progressive works as the *Cardinal Principles* report (Commission for the Reorganization of Secondary Education, 1918), the Eight-Year Study (Aiken, 1942), and some of the major reports of the Educational Policies Commission (1944, 1952). What made Hirsch's proposal different, however, was not the idea of common learning for social discourse and community cohesiveness, but the curricular means used to achieve the ends of discourse and community. Past progressive initiatives in general education were focused on learning that dealt with pervasive sociocivic problems framed with the intention of developing competencies for effective citizenship (e.g., the ability to think rationally and to express thoughts clearly, respect for other persons and other viewpoints, working cooperatively, using one's leisure time in socially useful ways). Hirsch's notion, on the other hand, was focused on specifying to the schools the precise elements of knowledge to be studied in the common curriculum. Thus the role of the curriculum was to transmit a preidentified body of knowledge to students for the purpose of engaging them in later conversation and debate. The major criticism of Hirsch's proposal centered around the prescriptive nature of his curriculum. His recipe-like approach to cultural literacy was reinforced by the publication of cultural literacy dictionaries, cultural literacy workbooks, and cultural literacy tests. Rather than valuing student dialogue, the common curriculum posed by Hirsch was criticized for valuing the acquisition of facts and for leading to reductive forms of teaching and assessment that seemed to contradict the general education spirit of problem-focused inquiry aimed at social insight. Still, despite what one might think about Hirsch's proposal, it is clear that the cultural literacy idea rekindled the debate over why a body of commonly shared understandings is essential to the vitality of a democracy and how such a concern should be integrated into the public school curriculum.

The importance of general education in the curriculum is underscored by the need for the school to merge learning with the idea of sharing and community participation. As Dewey (1916) stated, there is more than a linguistic tie between the words *common, community* and *communication*. Shared interests and outlooks form the moral basis of the society. This moral authority, however, is reflective in nature and is kept vital through the avenues of inquiry, discussion, criticism, and agitation. Minority viewpoints are included in public discussion and processes of inquiry; they contribute to both the modification and the solidification of the patterns of community and political life in the society.

The Experimental Mode of Thought in the Curriculum

Radicals have outlined the dangers of rampant rationality as it applies to the school curriculum. As mentioned, Dewey (1928) also made it clear that the procedures of science had to be approached modestly in the curriculum with an eye toward their abuse. Yet the method of science permeates the thought of pragmatists such as Dewey (1916), who once declared that the essentials of educational method are "identical with the essentials of reflection" (p. 163). This dictum led him to advance a problem-focused curriculum approach whose central purpose was to enable students to make intelligent decisions in problematic situations in experience. Such an approach assumed that the essential skills, appreciations, and knowledge of living were best developed and acquired through the process of scientific inquiry. The ability to make inferences, to engage in and understand persuasive argumentation, to inquiry into various claims and problems, and to exert intelligent control over one's life (and by implication, the collective life of one's community and society) were believed to be at the heart of an inquiry process that asked children to think in terms of actions that tested, revised, and expanded their ideas.

At the same time, the pragmatic tradition did not believe that the values of democracy could be engendered solely through the attitudes and skills inherent in the experimentalist mode of thought. As Childs (1956) argued, there are values that transcend those of the method of experimental inquiry, including the faith in the worth and dignity of individual human beings, the recognition of the principle of equality of treatment, and the belief in the resolution of conflict through cooperative means. These represent some of the binding forces of our social democratic condition transmitted to us through historical experience; as such, they also represent the axiological elements of pragmatism.

Thus, unlike critical theory, pragmatism does not engage in a continuous process of negativity against convention, tradition, and other forms of conservatism. Moreover, it views freedom not as the absence of external restraint, but as positive action built on the idea of teaching youth to deal with problematic situations through methods of analysis and techniques of cooperation and control. Obviously, pragmatists see the scientific method as leading to growth and change in experience, but these changes are accomplished through a process of intellectual inquiry and discussion. Thus the possibility of preserving, enriching, and transmitting certain group values and meanings is maintained.

To recover the experimental mode of thought in curriculum development does not mean that we have to put the wheels in motion for a management model of curriculum development that stresses a strategy of matching preordained goals to desired behaviors. In the pragmatic tradition, the term *rational* was equated with the idea of reflective and problem-focused thought. To Dewey, it was

> a manner of analyzing, "sizing up," projecting and testing hunches, observing results, making tentative generalizations, "having another try," prizing what one had come to value, [and] amending that value as required by change and critical appraisal (Wirth, 1989, p. 275).

In this way, the reconstruction of experience was secured, but in an investigatory context that also allowed for the preservation of common values and outlooks and for the potential treatment of certain phenomenological themes in the curriculum. As Wirth (1989) observed, the challenges offered by other traditions, including the existential and psychoanalytic, may still achieve some synthesis with the scientific–humanist orientation represented by Dewey, even though the current divisions are wide. This underscores the significance of the continuous challenge offered by curriculum scholars, such as William Pinar and C. A. Bowers, who are concerned with students' phenomenological culture in the school. It should be stressed, however, that pragmatism signifies a method of bringing the self-correcting process of experimental inquiry into the schools for the purpose of serving democracy in the sphere of group life. It has little philosophical sympathy for the significance of unconscious or irrational behavior; for the existential themes of meaninglessness, despair, anxiety, and alienation; or for the postcritical emphasis on individualistic concerns in the curriculum. The postmodern constructions of pragmatism provided by Cherryholmes (1988) and Rorty (1983), for instance, are actually in contradiction to Dewey, especially as they deemphasize the primacy of science and the scientific method in school action.

In sum, the experimental method of developing meaning and understanding in school is part of the larger scheme of pragmatism that involves an evolutionary view of change and a democratic view of associated living. These factors result in the presentation of a functional curriculum in which youth deliberate and test the scientific and moral meanings of experience in an effort to extend their powers of self-control and self-governance.

Deliberate Theory

Another step in recognizing Dewey's pragmatism in curriculum theory and development is facilitated by the distinction that Reid (1981) constructed between the role of "procedure" and the role of "method" in the curriculum. For Reid, the instrumentalist orientation is captured in the idea of curriculum procedure, which he notes to be an axiomatic form of reasoning that predetermines outcomes and operationalizes the school experience with a scientistic rationality that masquerades as common sense. However, the notion of "method" developed by Reid emerges not from a systems but from a deliberative orientation. Method, in this sense, retains a practical purpose; but rather than dictating the curriculum, it guides it in an open-ended way. According to Reid, Dewey's work is set in this perspective, as is the work of more contemporary curriculum scholars such as Schwab, Eisner, and Westbury. "Method in the curriculum", observed Reid, "allows for particularity, is under the control of people and regards them as acting in morally committed ways" (p. 174).

The difference between procedure and method in the curriculum is largely the difference between Bobbitt and Dewey; it is also the difference between Bobbitt and a number of "traditionalists," including Tyler, Taba, and the Tanners. Method is in the spirit of Dewey's pragmatism; it is the fabric upon which the divided nature of curriculum scholarship may begin to receive a mending.

SUMMARY

The increasingly unsteady conceptual foundation on which the American public school is based has been partly a function of the historical willingness of both radicals and conservatives to dismantle the common school structure of public education. Overlapping agendas supporting the individualization of schooling procedures have created an uneasy alliance between economic and cultural conservatives on the one hand and a variety of radical commentators on the other. The crisis of design among radicals has allowed their voice of protest to be coopted by those who are seeking to institute a differentiated educational system that will manifestly, not latently, serve the interests of those who are financially and politically empowered.

Since the design of the school curriculum is an act of defining education itself, it cannot be ignored or skirted. Design issues are crucial in making the most high-minded ideals of public schooling real and in offering answers to questions about the kind of society we hope to cultivate. The pragmatic tradition in curriculum development is one way for curriculum design to break free from behavioristic influences and to retain a sense of both particularity and community responsiveness in the school. At the same time, pragmatism provides a way for all public schools to blend scientific processes of inquiry with democratic processes of social mutuality and to express this blending in the learning activities of the school. Recovering the sociocivic role of the common school and the place of general education in the school curriculum are fundamental to the progressive-pragmatic hope for problem-focused learning devoted to the issues, concerns, and interests of a pluralistic democracy.

References

I

Adler, M. J. (1982). *The paideia proposal*. New York: Macmillan.

Aiken, W. (1942). *The story of the Eight-Year Study*. New York: Harper & Row.

Anderson, R. H. (1988). Political pressures on supervisors. In L. N. Tanner (Ed.), *Critical issues in curriculum* (pp. 60–82). Chicago: University of Chicago Press.

Anyon, J. (1981). Social class and school knowledge. *Curriculum Inquiry, 11*(1), 30–42.

Apple, M. W. (1979). *Ideology and curriculum*. London: Routledge & Kegan Paul.

Apple, M. W. (1981). Social structure, ideology and curriculum. In M. Lawn & L. Barton (Eds.), *Rethinking curriculum studies: A radical approach* (pp. 131–159). New York: Wiley.

Barrow, R. (1976). *Common sense and the curriculum*. Hamden, CT: Linnte Books.

Bennett, E. W. (1987). *James Madison High School*. Washington, DC: US Office of Education.

Bennett, K. P., & LeCompte, M. D. (1990). *How schools work: A sociological analysis of education*. White Plains, NY: Longman.

Bestor, A. E. (1953). *Educational wastelands*. Urbana: University of Illinois Press.

Bestor, A. E. (1956). *The restoration of learning*. New York: Knopf.

Bobbitt, J. F. (1913). *The supervision of city schools: Some general principles of management applied to the problems of city-school systems* (12th Yearbook of the National Society for the Study of Education, Part I). Bloomington, IL: Public School Publishing Co.

Bobbitt, J. F. (1918). *The curriculum*. Boston: Houghton Mifflin.

Bobbitt, J. F. (1924). *How to make a curriculum*. Boston: Houghton Mifflin.

Bode, B. H. (1927). *Modern educational theories*. New York: Macmillan.

Bode, B. H. (1935a). Dr. Bode replies. *The Social Frontier, 2*, 41–43.

Bode, B. H. (1935b). Education and social reconstruction. *The Social Frontier, 1*, 21.

Bode, B. H. (1938a). Dr. Childs and education for democracy. *The Social Frontier, 5*(39), 38–40.

Bode, B. H. (1938b). *Education at the crossroads*. New York: Newson & Company.

Bowers, C. A. (1984). *The promise of theory.* New York: Longman.

Bowers, C. A. (1987). *Elements of a post-liberal theory of education.* New York: Teachers College Press.

Bowers, C. A. (1991a). Some questions about the anachronistic elements in the Giroux/McLaren theory of critical pedagogy. *Curriculum Inquiry, 21*(2), 239–252.

Bowers, C. A. (1991b). Critical pedagogy and the "arch of social dreaming": A response to the criticism of Peter McLaren. *Curriculum Inquiry, 21*(4), 479–487.

Bowles, S., & Gintis, H. (1976). *Schooling in capitalist America.* New York: Basic Books.

Boyer, E. (1983). *High school.* New York: Harper & Row.

Brossard, C. (1967, May 30). Our most devastating critic. *Look, 31,* 75.

Burke, L. (1978, March). *Learning from the curricular past.* Paper presented at the American Educational Research Association, Toronto, Canada.

Callahan, R. E. (1962). *Education and the cult of efficiency.* Chicago: The University of Chicago Press.

Callahan, R. E. (1971). George S. Counts: Educational statesman. In R. J. Havighurst (Ed.), *Leaders in American education* (77th Yearbook of the National Society for the Study of Education, pp. 177–187). Chicago: University of Chicago Press.

Caswell, H. L., & Campbell, D. S. (1935). *Curriculum development.* New York: American Book Co.

Charters, W. W. (1924). *Curriculum construction.* New York: Macmillan Publishing Co.

Cherryholmes, C. (1988). *Power and criticism: Poststructural investigations in education.* New York: Teachers College Press.

Cherryholmes, C. (1992). Notes on pragmatism and scientific realism. *Educational Researcher, 21*(6), 13–17.

Childs, J. L. (1938). Dr. Bode on "authentic democracy." *The Social Frontier, 5*(39), 40–43.

Childs, J. L. (1956). *American pragmatism and education.* New York: Henry Holt and Co.

Chubb, J. E., & Moe, T. M. (1990). *Politics, markets and America's schools.* Washington, DC: Brookings Institute.

Coleman, J. S., Campbell, E. Q., Hobson, C. J., McPartland, J., Mood, A. M., Weinfeld, F. D., & York, R. L. (1966). *Equality of educational opportunity.* Washington, DC: Office of Education, U.S. Department of Health, Education and Welfare.

Commission for the Reorganization of Secondary Education. (1918). *Cardinal principles of secondary education.* Washington, DC: U.S. Government Printing Office.

Committee of the Progressive Association on Social and Economic Problems. (1933). *A call to the teachers of the nation.* New York: John Day Co.

Conant, J. B. (1959). *The American high school today.* New York: McGraw-Hill.

Coons, J. E., & Sugarman, S. D. (1978). *Education by choice: The case for family control.* Berkeley: University of California Press.

Counts, G. S. (1922). *The selective character of American secondary education.* Chicago: University of Chicago Press.

Counts, G. S. (1927). *The social composition of boards of education.* Chicago: University of Chicago Press.

Counts, G. S. (1928). *School and society in Chicago.* New York: Harcourt, Brace and Co.

Counts, G. S. (1930). *The American road to culture: A social interpretation of education in the United States.* New York: The John Day Co.

Counts, G. S. (1932). *Dare the schools build a new social order?* New York: The John Day Co.

Counts, G. S. (1935). Economics and the good life. *The Social Frontier, 2,* 72–73.

Cremin, L. A. (1955). The revolution in American secondary education. *Teachers College Record, 56,* 295–308.

Cremin, L. A. (1961). *The transformation of the school.* New York: Knopf.

Cuban, L. (1984). *How teachers taught: Constancy and change in American classrooms, 1890–1980.* New York: Longman.

Cuban, L. (1990). Reforming again and again and again. *Educational Researcher, 19*(1), 3–13.

Dewey, J. (1902a). *The child and the curriculum.* Chicago: University of Chicago Press.

Dewey, J. (1902b). *The school and society.* Chicago: University of Chicago Press.

Dewey, J. (1914). A policy of industrial education. *The New Republic, 1*(7), 11–12.

Dewey, J. (1915). Education v. trade-training—Dr. Dewey's reply. *The New Republic, 3,* 42–43.

Dewey, J. (1916). *Democracy and education.* New York: Macmillan.

Dewey, J. (1917a). The principle of nationality. In J. A. Boydston (Ed.), *John Dewey: The middle works* (Vol. 10, pp. 285–291). Carbondale: Southern Illinois University Press.

Dewey, J. (1917b). *Creative intelligence.* New York: Henry Holt and Co.

Dewey, J. (1922). *Human nature and conduct.* New York: The Modern Library.

Dewey, J. (1927). *The public and its problems.* New York: Henry Holt and Co.

Dewey, J. (1928). Progressive education and the science of education. In R. D. Archambault (Ed.), *John Dewey on education* (pp. 169–181). New York: Modern Library.

Dewey, J. (1929a). Individuality and experience. In R. D. Archambault (Ed.), *John Dewey on education* (pp. 149–156). New York: Modern Library.

Dewey, J. (1929b). *The quest for certainty.* New York: Putnam.

Dewey, J. (1934). Can education share in social reconstruction? *The Social Frontier, 1,* 12.

Dewey, J. (1938a). Education, democracy and socialized economy. *The Social Frontier, 5*(40), 71–73.

Dewey, J. (1938b). *Experience and education.* New York: Macmillan.

Dewey, J. (1939). *Freedom and culture.* New York: Macmillan.

Dewey, J., & Childs, J. L. (1933). The socioeconomic situation and education. In W. H. Kilpatrick (Ed.), *The educational frontier* (pp. 32–72). New York: Appleton-Century.

Dewey, J., & Dewey, E. (1915). *Schools of tomorrow.* New York: Dutton.

Doll, R. C. (1964). *Curriculum improvement: Decision-making and process.* Boston: Allyn & Bacon.

Drost, W. (1977). Social efficiency reexamined: The Dewey-Snedden controversy. *Curriculum Inquiry, 7*(1), 19–32.

Edmonds, R., Comer, J. M., Hall, W., Hill, R., McGehee, N., Reddick, L., Taylor, H. F., & Wright, S. (1973). A black response to Christopher Jencks' *Inequality* and other issues. *Harvard Educational Review, 43*(1), 76–91.

Educational Policies Commission. (1944). *Education for ALL American youth.* Washington, DC: National Education Association.

Educational Policies Commission. (1952). *Education for ALL American youth: A further look.* Washington, DC: National Education Association.

Egan, K. (1978). What is curriculum? *Curriculum Inquiry, 8*(1), 65–72.

Eisner, E. (1979). *The educational imagination.* New York: Macmillan.

English, F. W. (1980). Curriculum mapping. *Educational Leadership, 37*(7), 558–559.

English, F. W. (1983). Contemporary curriculum circumstances. In F. W. English (Ed.), *Fundamental Curriculum Decisions.* Alexandria, VA: Association for Supervision and Curriculum Development.

Feinberg, W. (1975). *Reason and rhetoric.* New York: Wiley.

Feinberg, W. (1989). Fixing the schools: The ideological turn. In H. Giroux & P. McLaren (Eds.), *Critical pedagogy, the state, and cultural struggle.* Albany, NY: SUNY Press.

Finn, C. (1991). *We must take charge.* New York: The Free Press.

Franklin, B. M. (1986). *Building the American community.* London: Falmer Press.

Friedman, M. (1962). *Capitalism and freedom.* Chicago: University of Chicago Press.

Friedman, M., & Friedman, R. (1980). *Free to choose.* New York: Harcourt Brace Jovanovich.

Friere, P. (1973). *The pedagogy of the oppressed.* New York: Seabury.

Gibson, R. (1986). *Critical theory and education.* London: Hodder & Stoughton.

Giles, H. H., McCutchen, S. P., & Zechiel, A. N. (1942). *Exploring the curriculum.* New York: Harper & Row.

Giroux, H. (1979). Toward a new sociology of curriculum. *Educational Leadership, 37*(3), 248–253.

Giroux, H. (1980). Critical theory and rationality in citizenship education. *Curriculum Inquiry, 10*(4), 329–366.

Giroux, H. (1981). *Ideology, culture, and the process of schooling.* Philadelphia: Temple University Press.

Giroux, H. (1983a). Theories of reproduction and resistance in the new sociology of education. *Harvard Educational Review, 53,* 257–293.

Giroux, H. (1983b). *Theory and resistance in education: A pedagogy for the opposition.* South Hadley, MA: Bergin & Garvey.

Giroux, H. (1984). Marxism and schooling: The limits of radical discourse. *Educational Theory, 34*(2), 113–135.

Giroux, H. (1988a). *Schooling the struggle for public life.* Minneapolis: University of Minnesota Press.

Giroux, H. (1988b). *Teachers as intellectuals.* Granby, MA: Bergin & Garvey.

Giroux, H. (1992). Educational leadership and the crisis of democratic government. *Educational Researcher, 21*(4), 4–11.

Giroux, H., & Aronowitz, S. (1985). *Education under siege.* South Hadley, MA: Bergin & Garvey.

Glatthorn, A. A. (1987). *Curriculum leadership.* Glenview, IL: Scott, Foresman.

Goodlad, J. I. (1966). *The changing school curriculum.* New York: Fund for the Advancement of Education.

Goodlad, J. I. (1976). Educational opportunity: The context and the reality. In *Facing the future: Issues in education and schooling* (J. S. Golub, Ed.). New York: McGraw-Hill.

Goodlad, J. I. (1984). *A place called school.* New York: McGraw-Hill.

Goodman, P. (1964). *Compulsory mis-education.* New York: Horizon.

Graubard, A. (1974). *Free the children: Radical reform and the free school movement.* New York: Vintage.

Greer, C. (1972). *The great school legend.* New York: Viking.

Grumet, M. (1981). Restitution and reconstruction of educational experience: An autobiographical method of curriculum theory. In M. Lawn & L. Barton (Eds.), *Rethinking curriculum studies: A radical approach* (pp. 115–130). New York: Wiley.

Gutek, G. (1984). *George Counts and American civilization.* Macon, GA: Mercer University Press.

Gutmann, A. (1987). *Democratic education.* Princeton, NJ: Princeton University Press.

Harvard Committee. (1945). *General education in a free society.* Cambridge, MA: Harvard University Press.

Havighurst, R. J. (1971). Prophets and scientists in education. In D. U. Levine & R. J. Havighurst (Eds.), *Farewell to schools?* Worthington, OH: Charles A. Jones Publishing.

Hentoff, N. (1966). *Our children are dying.* New York: Viking.

Hirsch, E. D. (1987). *Cultural literacy.* Boston: Houghton-Mifflin.

Hlebowitsh, P. S. (1990, April). *National education reports since midcentury: A curriculum analysis.* Paper presented at the annual meeting of the American Educational Research Association, Boston, MA.

Hlebowitsh, P. S. (1992). Critical theory versus curriculum theory: Rethinking the dialogue on Dewey. *Educational Theory, 42*(1), 69–82.

Holt, M. (1978). *The common curriculum.* London: Routledge & Kegan Paul.

Horkheimer, M. (1972). *Critical theory: Selected essays.* New York: Herder & Herder.

Huebner, D. (1975). Curricular language and classroom meaning. In W. Pinar (Ed.), *Curriculum theorizing: The reconceptualists* (pp. 217–236). Berkeley, CA: McCutchan.

Huebner, D. (1976). The moribund curriculum field: Its wake and our work. *Curriculum Inquiry, 6*(2), 153–167.

Husen, T. (1983). Are standards in the U.S. schools really lagging behind those in other countries? *Phi Delta Kappan, 64,* 455–461.

Illich, I. (1971). *Deschooling society.* New York: Harper & Row.

Jackson, P. (1968). *Life in classrooms.* New York: Holt, Rinehart & Winston.

Jackson, P. (1977). Beyond good and evil: Observations on the recent criticisms of schooling. *Curriculum Inquiry, 6*(4), 311–314.

Jackson, P. (1980). Curriculum and its discontents. *Curriculum Inquiry, 10*(2), 159–172.

James, W. (1907). *Pragmatism.* New York: Longmans, Green.

James, W. (1909). *The meaning of truth.* New York: Longmans, Green.

Jencks, C. (1972a). The education voucher report. In J. A. Mecklenburger & R. W. Hostrop (Eds.), *Education vouchers: From theory to Alum Rock* (pp. 151–221) Homewood, IL: ETC Publications.

Jencks, C. (1972b). *Inequality.* New York: Basic Books.

Jencks, C. (1972c). Interview by Donald W. Robinson, *Phi Delta Kappan, 54,* 256–258.

Jickling, B. (1988). Paradigms in curriculum development: Critical comments on the work of Tanner and Tanner. *Interchange, 19*(2), 41–49.

Karier, C. J. (1967). *The individual, society and education.* Urbana: University of Illinois Press.

Karier, C. J. (1976). The odd couple: Radical economics and liberal history [Essay-review of S. Bowles and H. Gintis, *Schooling in capitalist America.*] *Educational Studies, 7,* 185–193.

Katz, M. (1971). *Class, bureaucracy and schools.* New York: Praeger.

Kearns, D. T., & Doyle, D. P. (1988). *Winning the brain race.* San Francisco: ICS Press.

Kliebard, H. M. (1975a). Bureaucracy and curriculum history. In W. Pinar (Ed.), *Curriculum theorizing: The reconceptualists.* Berkeley, CA: McCutchan Publishing Corporation.

Kliebard, H. M. (1975b). Reappraisal: The Tyler rationale. In W. Pinar (Ed.), *Curriculum theorizing: The reconceptualists.* Berkeley, CA: McCutchan. [Originally published in *School Review* (February, 1970), 259–272]

Kliebard, H. M. (1986). *The struggle for the American curriculum.* New York: Routledge & Kegan Paul.

Kliebard, H. M. (1988). Fads, fashions, and rituals: The instability of curriculum change. In L. N. Tanner (Ed.), *Critical Issues in Curriculum* (87th Yearbook of the National Society for the Study of Education, Part 1, pp. 16–34). Chicago: The University of Chicago Press.

Kozol, J. (1967). *Death at an early age.* Boston: Houghton Mifflin.

Krug, E. A. (1950). *Curriculum planning.* New York: Harper and Brothers.

Krug, E. A. (1964). *The shaping of the American high school* [Vol. 1, 1880–1920]. Madison: University of Wisconsin Press.

Krug, E. A. (1972). *The shaping of the American high school* [Vol. 2, 1920–1941]. Madison: University of Wisconsin Press.

Marcuse, H. (1964). *One dimensional man.* Boston: Beacon.

Magnet schools: Critics worry that special status breeds new form of inequality. (1987, June 24). *Education Week,* p. C7.

McKinney, W. L., & Westbury, I. (1975). Stability and change: The public schools in Gary, Indiana, 1940–1970. In W. A. Reid & D. F. Walker, *Case Studies in Curriculum Change* (pp. 1–53). Boston: Routledge & Kegan Paul.

McLaren, P. (1989). *Life in schools.* New York: Longman.

McNeil, L. M. (1986). *Contradictions of control: School structure and school knowledge.* New York: Routledge.

McNeil, L. M. (1988). Contradictions of reform. *Phi Delta Kappan, 69,* 478–485.

Molnar, A., & Zahorik, J. A. (1977). *Curriculum theory.* Washington, DC: Association for Supervision and Curriculum Development.

Moore, D. R., & Davenport, S. (1990). The new improved sorting machine. In W. J. Boyd & H. J. Walberg (Eds.), *Choice in education: Issues and politics* (pp. 187–223). Chicago: National Society for the Study of Education.

Morris, C. (1970). *The pragmatic movement in American philosophy.* New York: Braziller.

Nasaw, D. (1979). *Schooled to order.* New York: Oxford University Press.

National Commission on Excellence in Education. (1983). *A nation at risk.* Washington, DC: U.S. Department of Education.

National Commission on the Reform of Secondary Education. (1973). *The reform of secondary education.* New York: McGraw-Hill.

National Panel on High School and Adolescent Education. (1976). *The education of adolescents.* Washington, DC: U.S. Government Printing Office.

National Science Board. (1983). *Educating Americans for the twenty-first century.* Washington, DC: National Science Foundation.

Neill, A. S. (1962). *Summerhill.* New York: Hart.

Newlon, J. H. (1939a). Are we growing up politically? *The Social Frontier, 5*(46), 262–264.

Newlon, J. H. (1939b). *Education for democracy in our times.* New York: McGraw-Hill.

Oakes, J. (1985). *Keeping track: How schools structure inequality.* New Haven, CT: Yale University Press.

Panel on Youth of the President's Science Advisory Committee. (1974). *Youth: Transition to adulthood.* Chicago: University of Chicago Press.

Pauley, E. (1991). *The classroom crucible.* New York: Basic Books.

Pinar, W. F. (1975). *Curriculum theorizing: The reconceptualists.* Berkeley, CA: McCutchan.

Pinar, W. F. (1978). Notes on the curriculum field 1978. *Educational Researcher, 7*(8), 5–12.

Pinar, W. F. (1980). A reply to my critics. *Curriculum Inquiry, 10*(2), 199–205.

Pinar, W. F. (1988). *Contemporary curriculum discourses.* Scottsdale, AZ: Gorsuch Scarbrick.

Pinar, W. F., & Bowers, C. A. (1992). Politics of curriculum: Origins, controversies and significant critical perspectives. In G. Grant (Ed.), *Review of research in education* (pp. 163–190). Washington DC: American Educational Research Association.

Pinar, W. F., & Grumet, M. (1981). Theory and practice and the reconceptualisation of curriculum studies. In M. Lawn & L. Barton (Eds.), *Rethinking curriculum studies: A radical approach* (pp. 20–42). New York: Wiley.

Popham, W. J., & Baker E. L. (1970). *Establishing instructional goals.* Englewood Cliffs, NJ: Prentice-Hall.

Presseisen, B. Z. (1985). *Unlearned lessons.* Philadelphia: Falmer.

Ravitch, D. (1977). *The revisionists revised: A critique of the radical attack on the schools.* New York: Basic Books.

Raywid, M. A. (1984). Synthesis of research on school choice. *Educational Leadership, 41*(7), 71–78.

Reid, W. A. (1975). The changing curriculum: Theory and practice. In W. A. Reid & D. F. Walker (Eds.), *Case Studies in Curriculum Change* (pp. 240–259). London: Routledge & Kegan Paul.

Reid, W. A. (1981). The deliberate approach to the study of the curriculum. In M. Lawn & L. Barton (Eds.), *Rethinking curriculum studies: A radical approach* (pp. 160–187). New York: Wiley.

Reimers, E. (1971). *School is dead.* Garden City, NY: Doubleday.

Rickover, H. G. (1959). *Education and freedom.* New York: Dutton.

Rorty, R. (1983). *Consequences of pragmatism.* Minneapolis: University of Minnesota Press.

Ross, E. A. (1901). *Social control.* New York: Macmillan.

Rugg, H. O. (Ed.). (1927). *The foundations of curriculum-making* (26th yearbook of the NSSE). Bloomington, IL: National Society for the Study of Education.

Saylor, G., & Alexander, W. M. (1966). *Curriculum planning for modern schools.* New York: Holt, Rinehart & Winston.

Schubert, W. H. (1986). *Curriculum: Perspective, paradigm and possibility.* New York: Macmillan.

Schubert, W. H. (1987). Educationally recovering Dewey in the curriculum. *Current Issues in Education, 7,* 1–32.

Schubert, W. H., Posner, G. J., & Schubert, A. L. (1982). Professional preferences of curriculum scholars: A genealogical study; cited in W. H. Schubert (1987), Educationally recovering Dewey in the curriculum, *Current Issues in Education, 7,* 1–32.

Schwab, J. J. (1970). *The practical: The language for curriculum.* Washington, DC: National Education Association.

Schwab, J. J. (1978). The practical: A language for curriculum. In I. Westbury & N. J. Wilkof (Eds.), *Science, curriculum and liberal education* (pp. 287–321). Chicago: University of Chicago Press.

Seguel, M. L. (1966). *The curriculum field: Its formative years.* New York: Teachers College Press.

Shaker, P. (1991). Curriculum anomaly. *Journal of Curriculum and Supervision, 6*(2), 167–177.

Shane, H. G. (1981). Significant writings that have influenced the curriculum. *Phi Delta Kappan, 62,* 311–314.

Shor, I. (1986). *Culture wars: School and society in the conservative restoration, 1969–1984.* Boston: Routledge & Kegan Paul.

Shulman, L. S. (1987). Knowledge and teaching: Foundations of the new reform. *Harvard Educational Review, 57*(1), 1–27.

Sizer, T. R. (1972). The case for a free market. In J. A. Mecklenburger & R. W. Hostrop (Eds.), *Education vouchers: From theory to Alum Rock* (pp. 24–32). Homewood, IL: ETC Publications.

Sizer, T. R. (1984). *Horace's compromise.* Boston: Houghton Mifflin.

Slavin, R. E. (1987). The Hunterization of American schools. *Instructor, 96,* 56–58.

Smith, B. O., Stanley, W. O., & Shores, J. H. (1957). *Fundamentals of curriculum development.* New York: Harcourt Brace Jovanovich.

Snedden, D. (1914). Vocational education. *The New Republic, 3,* 40–42.

Spring, J. (1972). *Education and the rise of the corporate state.* Boston: Beacon.

Spring, J. (1988). *Conflict of interest.* New York: Longman.

Taba, H. (1945). General techniques for curriculum planning. In N. B. Nelson (Ed.), *American education in the postwar period: Curriculum reconstruction* (44th Yearbook of the NSSE, Part 1, pp. 80–115). Chicago: University of Chicago Press.

Taba, H. (1962). *Curriculum development: Theory and practice.* New York: Harcourt, Brace & World.

Tanner, D. (1974). The retreat from education—for other people's children. *Intellect, 102,* 222–225.

Tanner, D. (1982). Curriculum history. In *Encyclopedia of Educational Research.* New York: Macmillan and The Free Press.

Tanner, D. (1986). Are reforms like swinging pendulums? In H. J. Walberg & J. W. Keefe (Eds.), *Rethinking reform: The principal's dilemma* (pp. 5–18). Reston, VA: National Association of Secondary School Principals.

Tanner, D., & Tanner, L. N. (1979). Emancipation from research: The reconceptualist prescription. *Educational Researcher, 8*(6), 8–12.

Tanner, D., & Tanner, L. N. (1980). *Curriculum development: Theory into practice* (2nd ed.). New York: Macmillan.

Tanner, D., & Tanner, L. N. (1990). *The history of the school curriculum.* New York: Macmillan.

Task Force on Education for Economic Growth. (1983). *Action for excellence.* Washington, DC: Education Commission of the States.

Thayer, H. S. (1968). *Meaning and action: A critical history of pragmatism.* Indianapolis: Hackett.

Tyler, R. W. (1949). *Basic principles of curriculum and instruction.* Chicago: University of Chicago Press.

Tyler, R. W. (1966). New dimensions in curriculum development. *Phi Delta Kappan, 48*(1), 25–28.

Tyler, R. W. (1973). The father of behavioral objectives criticizes them: An interview with Ralph Tyler. *Phi Delta Kappan, 55*(1), 55–57.

Tyler, R. W. (1981). Specific approaches to curriculum development. In H. A. Giroux, A. N. Pena, & W. F. Pinar (Eds), *Curriculum and instruction: Alternatives in education* (pp. 17–30). Berkeley, CA: McCutchan.

Tyler, R. W. (1984). Personal reflections on The Practical 4. *Curriculum Inquiry, 14*(1), 97–102.

Vallance, E. (1973). Hiding the hidden curriculum: An interpretation of the justification in nineteenth-century educational reform. *Curriculum Theory Network, 4*(1), 5–21.

Weinberg, J. (1972). *Edward Alsworth Ross.* Madison: State Historical Society of Wisconsin.

What schools cannot do. (1972, September 18). *Time*, pp. 41–42.

Willis, G. (1975). Curriculum theory and the context of the curriculum. In W. F. Pinar (Ed.), *Curriculum theorizing: The reconceptualists* (pp. 427–444). Berkeley, CA: McCutchan.

Wirth, A. G. (1989). *John Dewey as educator: His design for work in education (1894–1904).* Lanham, MD: University Press of America.

Wraga, W. G. (1991). *The comprehensive high school in the United States since midcentury.* Unpublished doctoral dissertation, Rutgers University, New Brunswick, NJ.

Index

About the Author

Peter S. Hlebowitsh is an assistant professor in the Division of Curriculum and Instruction at the University of Iowa. His more recent publications have appeared in *Educational Theory*, *Journal of Curriculum Studies*, and *Science Education*. From 1989 to 1993, he co-directed the graduate program in Curriculum Studies at the University of Houston. He is the editor of the John Dewey Society's journal, *Current Issues in Education*, and is a member of the editorial board of the *Journal of Educational Thought*. His research interests are in the areas of curriculum history, curriculum theory, teacher education, and educational policy.